THE JOB BOOK II
100 Day Jobs
For Actors

Smith and Kraus *Books For Actors*

THE MONOLOGUE SERIES

The Best Men's / Women's Stage Monologues of 1994
The Best Men's / Women's Stage Monologues of 1993
The Best Men's / Women's Stage Monologues of 1992
The Best Men's / Women's Stage Monologues of 1991
The Best Men's / Women's Stage Monologues of 1990
One Hundred Men's / Women's Stage Monologues from the 1980's
2 Minutes and Under: Character Monologues for Actors
Street Talk: Character Monologues for Actors
Uptown: Character Monologues for Actors
Monologues from Contemporary Literature: Volume I
Monologues from Classic Plays
100 Great Monologues from the Renaissance Theatre
100 Great Monologues from the Neo-Classical Theatre
100 Great Monologues from the 19th C. Romantic and Realistic Theatres
Ice Babies In Oz: Original Character Monologues

FESTIVAL MONOLOGUE SERIES

The Great Monologues from the Humana Festival
The Great Monologues from the EST Marathon
The Great Monologues from the Women's Project
The Great Monologues from the Mark Taper Forum

YOUNG ACTORS SERIES

Great Scenes and Monologues for Children
New Plays from A.C.T.'s Young Conservatory
Great Scenes for Young Actors from the Stage
Great Monologues for Young Actors
Multicultural Monologues for Young Actors
Multicultural Scenes for Young Actors

SCENE STUDY SERIES

Scenes From Classic Plays 468 B.C. to 1960 A.D.
The Best Stage Scenes of 1994
The Best Stage Scenes of 1993
The Best Stage Scenes of 1992
The Best Stage Scenes for Men / Women from the 1980's

CONTEMPORARY PLAYWRIGHTS SERIES

Romulus Linney: 17 Short Plays
Eric Overmyer: Collected Plays
Lanford Wilson: 21 Short Plays
William Mastrosimone: Collected Plays
Horton Foote: 4 New Plays
Israel Horovitz: 16 Short Plays
Terrence McNally: 15 Short Plays
Humana Festival '93: The Complete Plays
Humana Festival '94: The Complete Plays
Women Playwrights: The Best Plays of 1992
Women Playwrights: The Best Plays of 1993

CAREER DEVELOPMENT SERIES

Anne Bogart: Viewpoints
The Smith and Kraus Monologue Index
What To Give Your Agent For Christmas & 100 Other Tips for the Working Actor
The Camera Smart Actor
The Sanford Meisner Approach
The Actor's Chekhov
Kiss and Tell: Restoration Scenes, Monologues, & History
Cold Readings: Some Do's and Don'ts for Actors at Auditions

If you require pre-publication information about upcoming Smith and Kraus books, you may receive our semi-annual catalogue, free of charge, by sending your name and address to *Smith and Kraus Catalogue, P.O. Box 127, One Main Street, Lyme, NH 03768. Or call us at (800) 895-4331, fax (603) 795-4427.*

the
JOB BOOK II
100 Day Jobs
For Actors

by Glenn Alterman

A Career Development Book

SK
A Smith and Kraus Book

Published by Smith and Kraus, Inc.
One Main Street, Lyme, NH 03768

Copyright © 1995 by Smith and Kraus, Inc.
All rights reserved
Manufactured in the United States of America
Cover and Text Design by Julia Hill
Cover photo ©1995 by

First Edition: November 1995
10 9 8 7 6 5 4 3 2 1

Library of Congress Cataloging-in-Publication

Alterman, glenn, 1946-

    The Job Book II: 100 day jobs for actors / by Glenn Alterman.

    p. cm. --(a career development book)

    ISBN 1-880399-99-7

    1. Acting--vocational guidance. 2. Performing arts--vocational guidance. I. Title. II. title: 100 day jobs for actors. iv. Series.

    PN2055.A45   1994

    792'.028'023   94-46978

                          CIP

For
Spider Duncan Christopher

BIOGRAPHY

Glenn Alterman is the author of *Street Talk, Uptown, Two Minutes and Under, The Job Book: 100 Acting Jobs for Actors, Beginnings: Monologues of the Stars* and *What to Give Your Agent for Christmas and 100 Other Tips for the Working Actor*, all for Smith and Kraus. *Street Talk* and *Uptown* were the #1 best selling books of the original monologue collections in 1992 and 1993, and along with *The Job Book: 100 Acting Jobs for Actors*, were featured selections in the Doubleday Book Club (Fireside Theater). *Two Minutes and Under* recently went into its second printing. His play *Like Family* was optioned by Red Eye Pictures (with Alterman writing the screen-play). *Nobody's Flood* won The Bloomington National Playwriting Competition (and was a finalist at the Key West Theater Festival). He wrote the book for *Heartstrings—The National Tour* (commissioned by the Design Industries Foundation for Aids). His "monologue" plays include *Kiss Me When It's Over* (commissioned by E. Weissman Productions), *Tourists of the Mindfield* (semi-finalist in the L. Arnold Weissberger Playwriting Competition at New Dramatists produced by the West Bank Cafe Downstairs Theater), and *Street Talk/Uptown*, based on his books (produced at the West Coast Ensemble in Los Angeles). *Goin' Round on Rock Solid Ground*, his first "dialogue" play, was a finalist at the Actors Theater of Louisville (workshop productions at Circle Rep Lab and The West Bank Cafe). *Spilt Milk*, which received its premiere at Beverly Hills Rep (Theater 40), was selected to participate in the Samuel French One-Act Play Festival. *The Danger of Strangers* recently received a fully staged reading in the Pittsburgh New Works Festival and was a finalist in the George R. Kernodle Contest. His plays have also been performed at Primary Stages, HOME (Tiny Mythic Theater), in the Turnip Festival, at Playwrights Horizons, La Mama, and on Theater Row in New York.

Contents

Introduction x

Acting Career Consultant 2
Actor Label Service 3
Administrative Assistant 4
Animal Trainer and Groomer 5
Answering Service Operator (Telephone Secretary) 6
Apartment and Closet Organizer 7
Arborist 8
Astrologer 9
Audiovisual Coordinator 10
Bank Teller 11
Bellhop 12
Bookmobile Driver 13
Braille Word Processor 14
Building Custodian (Janitor) 15
Campaign Worker 16
Canvas Sampler 17
Car Rental Clerk 18
Card Reader (Fortune-telling) 19
Carpenter 20
Carpet Installer 21
Cashier 22
Cat Sitter (House Sitter) 23
Census Taker 24
Civics Instructor 25

Coat Check Attendant. 26
College Basketball Referee 27
Computer Consultant. 28
Cook. 29
Cosmetologist And Barber. 30
Counter Clerk. 31
Croupier. 32
Customer Representative 33
Deckhand On A Schooner
   (Or Other Tall-Masted Sailing Ship) 34
Dispatcher 35
File Clerk 36
Flea Market Operator 37
Flight Attendant 38
Flyer and Brochure Distributor. 39
Food Stylist 40
Foreign Language Teacher 41
Freelance Fund-raiser. 42
Gardener 43
Greeter (For Hotel Dining Rooms and Restaurants). 44
Hand Model 45
Health Club Receptionist 46
Host/Hostess for New York Skyride 47
Hotel (and Motel) Desk Clerk 48
Housepainter 49
Hypnotist 50
Indexer. 51
Job Developer. 52
Library Technical Assistant 53
Lifeguard 54
Mail Clerk. 55
Market Research Group 56
Massage Therapist 57
Member of a Yacht Crew. 58
Messenger 59
Murder Mystery Actor. 60
Paperhanger. 61
Patient Advocate. 62
Performer's Tax Consultant. 63
Personal Assistant 64

Personal Trainer 65
Plasterer 66
Playing Superheroes 67
Postal Clerk and Mail Carrier 68
Preschool Worker 69
Program Director for Charity Organizations 70
Proofreader 71
Public Opinion Poll Taker 72
Public Relations Assistant at the Library 73
Real Estate Agent 74
Receiving, Traffic and Shipping Clerk 75
Receptionist 76
Recruiter/Executive Search Research 77
Repo Man 78
Retail Salesperson 79
Sailmaker 80
Security Officer (Guard) 81
Shopper/Spotter 82
Sperm Donor (Men Only) 83
Substitute Schoolteacher 84
Teacher's Aide 85
Teaching English as a Second Language 86
Telemarketer 87
Theater Technical Director 88
Theater Ticket Order Taker 89
Tile Setter 90
Timekeeping and Payroll Clerk 91
Tour Guide 92
Toy Demonstrator 93
Translator 94
Travel Agent 95
Tutor 96
Vocational Assessment Coordinator 97
Waiter 98
White-Water Rafting Guide 99
Wine Steward (Sommeliers) 100
Wire Transfer Worker 101
Yoga Instructor (Private and Group) 102

INTRODUCTION

The overwhelming response to *The Job Book: 100 Acting Jobs for Actors* was certainly proof that job opportunity books for actors are very much needed today. Realizing that there's a gold mine of opportunities for actors should be of real consolation to those struggling just to make ends meet.

While working on this book, I've discovered that not only are there jobs out there—but good ones, well paying ones, jobs suitable for an actor's lifestyle and needs. I've tried to give a healthy sampling from all areas of the job market, from office work to construction, to artistic, to offbeat. I believe there's something for everyone in this book, a job for every actor's taste and disposition. I rejected potential jobs that were not compatible to an actor's needs for auditions, showcases, classes, theatre and movie work. I also weeded out jobs that I felt didn't compensate enough for the time or energy required. I always kept in mind that this is a book written especially for actors.

Before sending this manuscript to my publisher, I passed around copies to several groups of actors in New York and Los Angeles and asked for their honest opinions and recommendations. With only a few job exceptions (which have been corrected) the book received overwhelming raves. I feel confident that *The Job Book II: 100 Day Jobs for Actors* will do as well, if not better than its companion. And I also feel that it offers every actor the best job opportunities around.

Glenn Alterman
Summer 1995

THE JOB BOOK II
100 Day Jobs
For Actors

Acting Career Consultant

Low Down

The acting career consultant gives advice and guidance to actors starting out in show business. Through one-on-one consultations they answer questions, provide insights and act out business role-playing scenarios with the actor.

Scratch

Generally $100 for a two-hour session.

Be
- Knowledgeable about all aspects of show business
- Caring about actors
- Willing to provide constant, ongoing support
- A good communicator and teacher

Perks
- Fulfilling when actors move up the ladder
- The money is good
- Flexible hours
- Work from your home

Bummers
- You have to deal with all types of actors and their neuroses
- You must always be available to answer questions and handle problems that may come up for the actor
- There are initial expenses (advertising, promotion)
- It takes a while to build up a clientele

Horse's Mouth

Sue Henderson, an actress who operates Sue Henderson Assoc., an actor consultation company: "There is no greater joy for me than to see an actor I've been working with really take off. One thing you must know about this kind of work is that you're almost always on call. Actors have varied schedules. Some work days, some work nights, some can only meet on Sunday, it all depends. You must be very flexible."

Contact

This is self-starter kind of work. Put up signs, send out flyers, advertise in *Backstage*. Reputation and word of mouth is how you build up a clientele. Sue Henderson has offered to assist beginning consultants with advice; tel. (212) 472-2292.

Actor Label Service

Low Down

Actor labels are computer printed labels that offer actors the names and addresses of casting directors, agents, model agencies, production houses, and regional theaters. When the actor wishes to correspond with any of these people they purchase the specific labels. This saves the actor a lot of time and footwork.

Scratch

Varies each month. Generally about $500 a month.

Be
- Organized
- Able to ascertain pertinent information on the phone on a monthly basis
- Good with a computer
- A good businessperson, capable of selling the labels and distributing them to stores on a monthly basis

Perks
- You get the updated information first and can use it to get your own acting work
- You work out of your home
- Aside from the few long days at the beginning of the month, you have the rest of the month free
- You have an ongoing relationship with casting directors, agents and production houses which can be beneficial to your own career

Bummers
- Tremendously time consuming. Must be willing to update the labels every month (three or four 12-16 hour days a month)
- Initial expenses such as buying a computer, getting labels, large phone bills and advertising
- Dealing with disgruntled actors who (very rarely, hopefully) find a mistake on the labels
- Business problems that come up in dealing with bookstores (running out of stock, bill payment, etc.)

Horse's Mouth

Sue Henderson, an actress who runs Sue Henderson Assoc., a label-making company: "With this type of work you have to be willing to constantly update on a monthly basis. You can't slack off, even once! This work can be very time consuming and demanding, especially when you're first starting out."

Contact

This is self-starter kind of work. Sue Henderson of Sue Henderson Assoc. has offered to assist anyone interested in learning about it; tel. (212) 472-2292. You may also call her if you're interested in ordering labels.

Administrative Assistant

Low Down

The administrative assistant's job is determined by the company he (she) works for. Each company has specific needs. Essentially however, the administrative assistant answers phones, sends and receives faxes, prepares invoices, facilitates communication with clients, schedules interviews, handles office correspondence, orders supplies, and handles the petty cash.

Scratch

$10-$20 an hour, depending on ability and experience.

Be
• Open and flexible
• Excellent on the phone
• Organized
• Able to use a computer (WordPerfect 5.0 a must!) and fax
• Able to run an office
• Tactful and professional

Perks
• Work can be challenging
• Interrelate with many people on a daily basis
• Good chance for advancement
• A lot of responsibility

Bummers
• Management can be difficult
• Pressure on the job
• Irate clients
• This type of work can be difficult to manage along with an acting career

Horse's Mouth

Arnold Zimmerman, actor: "I worked for a company downtown for about six months. I enjoyed it, but I have a tremendous amount of energy. The average guy may not have been able to do it. It wasn't that the work was physically demanding, but they always had me going. That could have just been that office. They were very busy. Eventually I got a road company job and left."

Contact

The best place to find this work is the Actors Work Program at Equity or the SAG board. One company that hires actors as administrative assistants is Callaghan Assoc., 119 West 57th Street, Suite 1220, New York, NY 10019; tel. (212) 265-9200.

Animal Trainer and Groomer

Low Down

This is for those actors who love working with all sorts of animals. Dog obedience training particularly has become a large growing field today. The basics can be learned in about five months. Aside from teaching animal obedience classes, trainers earn extra income by breeding dogs, running boarding kennels, and distributing pet care products. Generally most dog groomers are in business for themselves. Actors can find part-time work assisting in these small operations.

Scratch

- Groomers – varies, but usually get between $12-$30 an hour
- Trainers – varies, but usually $15-$25 an hour

Be

- An animal lover
- Comfortable disciplining animals
- Willing to start off by cleaning kennels

Perks

- If you like animals this is the work for you
- If you get into training animals for TV and film, the money can be excellent
- Great sense of accomplishment after an animal has been taught to do a trick or obey a command
- The sense of accomplishment when you've transformed that mangy mutt into an attractive-looking, well-groomed pet

Bummers

- Animals bite and scratch
- Owners are demanding
- There is the initial expense of classes to learn how to groom and train animals
- You may become attached to the animals

Horse's Mouth

Evelyn Reingold, an actress: "I've trained and groomed dogs for about seven years now. Five or six of the dogs I trained booked national commercials. It was such a thrill seeing them on TV. And yes, I wish I'd have booked one of those spots myself."

Contact

To train: The New York School of Dog Grooming, 248 East 34th Street, New York, NY 10016. For work: Try magazines like *Dog World* or the Yellow Pages.

Answering Service Operator (Telephone Secretary)

Low Down
Answering services hire operators (secretaries) to answer calls for their clients. When a message comes in the operator records pertinent information and places the message in a client's box. Then either a calling operator tries to reach the client to give him his message or the client calls in to receive his messages.

Scratch
$5 to $8 an hour.

Be
• A person equipped with "a smile in your voice"
• Equipped with legible handwriting
• A good communicator
• Personable

Perks
• You hear what's happening in the business
• You work in a theatrical environment
• Employers are actor-friendly
• Flexible hours

Bummers
• Tired voice
• Back and shoulder strain
• Poor pay

Horse's Mouth
Gordon Marra, president of Talent Exchange for 43 years (also owns On Board, Stand By, Encore, On Call, 7 Lively Arts, and Bells Are Ringing Answering Service): "One thing I recommend to all actors is that before signing on with any answering service see how long they've been in business. You may regret giving your business to an inexperienced company that may go out of business shortly after you sign with them. As for what I look for when hiring? I look for someone who is personable and has a smile in his or her voice."

Contact
Gordon Marra at any of the answering services previously mentioned; tel. (212) 265-5000.

Apartment and Closet Organizer

Low Down

In this type of work you come into people's homes and offices and help organize various spaces for them. The work may include helping to set up closets, cleaning out rooms and discarding unnecessary items.

Scratch

About $50-$80 per session. Generally takes from three to five sessions per client.

Be
- Well organized
- Able to communicate clearly
- Sensitive to people's need to hold on to things
- Blessed with good sense of space
- Neat and tidy

Perks
- Seeing homes or offices transformed
- Very challenging
- Very grateful clients

Bummers
- Some people are not willing to let go of their belongings no matter what
- Difficult clients
- Some clients discontinue after the first session

Horse's Mouth

Elyse Jolly, an actress: "I love doing this work. There are so many rewards in helping people clear out their apartments. It's really about letting go, something your clients are occasionally reluctant to do. When they do however, you can see them transform right before your eyes."

Contact

This is truly self-starter kind of work. When you're ready just put up signs on bulletin boards, place ads in local papers. Much of this work comes by word of mouth.

Arborist

Low Down
The term arborist includes several jobs, all of whose purpose is to keep trees healthy. Arborists used to be called "tree surgeons." Actors frequently do this work during the summer when auditions are slow and they want to be outdoors:

- Estimator – To keep a landowner's trees at their peak the estimator visits the location, determines the best course of action and estimates the cost of fertilizing, pruning, and insect control.
- Tree Planter – Usually travel to sites in groups. A group may stay together for up to six months. They are hired by logging companies. A good planter can plant about 3,000 trees a day.
- Tree Climbing Arborist – Actually climb trees to examine them and then make specific recommendations.

Scratch
Estimator, $25,000-$100,000 per year; Tree Climber, $6-$16 per hour; Tree Planter, $100-$125 per day.

Be
- A nature lover
- In good shape
- Willing to work for several weeks or months on end
- Knowledgeable about climbing ropes, chemical sprays and the use of different types of saws
- A college graduate in forestry for estimator work

Perks
- Wonderful outdoor work
- Work when available
- Estimators make very good money
- Camaraderie among work crews

Bummers
- Work can be dangerous
- May be working in inclement weather
- Chemical sprays are hazardous

Horse's Mouth
Lyle Ennerlind, an actor: "When I first got to New York, if I wasn't doing summer stock and had no summer plans, I'd take a month or two off and just work outdoors. For me it was like a "work vacation." And come September I'd be revved up and ready for auditions."

Contact
Superior Forest Services, Route 85, Leslie, AR 72645.

Astrologer

Low Down

Astrology readers ascertain the month, day, year, and exact time and place of a client's birth. They find out what the "skies" were like the first moment he (or she) took a breath. This information gives the astrologer a blueprint of the client's life. The chart is then progressed up to the day of the reading and the astrologer reveals to the client information about his life, past and future.

Scratch

Varies, anywhere from $75-$400 a reading.

Be
- An expert astrologer
- Knowledgeable as to the correct way to set up a horoscope
- A person with excellent communication skills
- Sensitive to people

Perks
- You meet all sorts of interesting people
- You develop a special intimacy with people
- Travel
- You can make a difference in people's lives
- The money can be very good
- Only do readings when you're available

Bummers
- Clients don't always keep their appointments
- Takes awhile to build up a clientele and a reputation
- At the beginning you have the initial expense of advertising and promotion

Horse's Mouth

Spider Duncan Christopher, an actor who is also a professional astrologer: "Being able to help other actors plan their careers has been a wonderful part of this type of work. I was asked to chart the opening night for a show once (The Best Little Whorehouse in Texas). The original opening night was changed because it was determined that it wouldn't be a good night astrologically. The show opened on a different night and was a major hit."

Contact

(For training) New York Astrology Center, 63 West 38th Street, New York, NY 10018. Spider Duncan Christopher is willing to train; tel. (212) 246-7684.

Audiovisual Coordinator

Low Down

ACs coordinate all the daily audiovisual needs of a company. A presentation may require a tape recorder, slide projector or movie projector. It's the AC's responsibility to have the machine ready to go at the appointed time in the assigned room. During the presentation the AC assists the leader as needed. After the presentation the AC returns the equipment to its proper place.

Scratch

$10-$15 an hour.

Be

- Knowledgeable about a wide array of audiovisual machinery
- Quick to learn to use new equipment
- Able to quickly and quietly set up and break down the equipment
- Able to assist in a presentation without being obtrusive
- Able to work comfortably in a corporate situation
- Competent in providing consultation and recommendation to anyone in the company needing advice about audiovisual machines
- Computer literate
- An excellent communicator

Perks

- Participation in high level corporate activities
- Opportunity to network in a company

Bummers

- Equipment breakdown puts AC on the spot
- Sometimes AC must delegate responsibility to under-qualified people who may mishandle and damage equipment
- Some presentations are made under a lot of pressure

Horse's Mouth

Ivan Bellini, an actor: "Being part of a successful sales presentation is very rewarding. Everyone from the CEOs to the pitchman get to know you sooner or later. On some presentations you work very closely with them and it's important that you get everything to work exactly right. You're an integral part of the presentation. It can be very exciting."

Contact

Most companies hire audiovisual coordinators on a full- or part-time basis. A lot of temp agencies also hire for this type of work. One such agency that does is Taylor Hodson, Inc., Staffing Services; tel. (212) 725-8429.

Bank Teller

Low Down
Bank tellers handle a wide range of banking business including check cashing and deposits. Usually the teller's day begins before the bank opens and continues after it closes. More and more bank tellers are being trained in customer service, the area many actors prefer because of the social skills required. In customer service the representative discusses the various services which the bank offers.

Scratch
Varies, depending on the bank, location and your experience. Generally about $9 an hour (on a part-time basis).

Be
- Good with figures and money
- At least a high school grad (with accounting, bookkeeping, economics and mathematics courses)
- Happy with public contact
- Computer literate
- Mature and tactful

Perks
- On a part-time basis the hours are flexible
- Good chance for advancement
- Good working conditions

Bummers
- Can be boring, repetitive work
- On your feet a lot
- Irate customers
- Must be constantly alert (dealing with money)

Horse's Mouth
Jan Duncan, an actress: "When I started doing customer service for the bank the job became interesting. Although I've always been good with figures it was the people part of bank telling I liked most."

Contact
The best way to get this kind of work is to contact the bank you want to work for. To learn more about this field contact: American Bankers Assoc., Reference Library, 1120 Connecticut Avenue NW, Washington, DC 20036.

Bellhop

Low Down

A bellhop works in a hotel or guest house and carries the guests' bags to their rooms, delivers messages, food (sometimes), runs errands, assists handicapped persons, delivers ice, directs people to their destinations and handles other chores as determined by the management.

Scratch

Varies widely, depending on which hotel, if union or non-union, what shift, and how good the tips are. Generally a bellhop makes between $100 and $300 per shift (including tips).

Be
- Strong
- Polite
- Friendly
- Neat
- Courteous

Perks
- If you work for a good hotel and get the best shift you can make excellent money
- Free meals
- Meet all kinds of people

Bummers
- Rude hotel guests
- Small tips
- Backbreaking work
- Management that is difficult to work for

Horse's Mouth

Chris Nelson, a dancer who worked at the New York Athletic Club: "This work just wasn't for me. I felt like I was a servant. It's not that the people weren't nice, it's just the nature of the job didn't suit me. The money, however, was very good."

Contact

Chris Nelson suggested looking through the want ads in the New York Times, which is where he found his job. Alternatively, contact the personnel office of the hotel you'd like to work for.

Bookmobile Driver

Low Down

To make library services available to wide audiences of people many libraries hire drivers to drive bookmobiles through various neighborhoods. The vans are stocked with all sorts of library materials, books, magazines, records and cassettes. The vans visit shopping centers, nursing homes, apartment complexes and schools. The bookmobile driver, like the librarian, answers questions, checks books in and out, collects fees on late books and re-shelves books.

Scratch

Depends on location. Generally between $8 and $13 an hour.

Be
- Equipped with librarian skills
- A licensed driver
- Willing to assist handicapped, blind and elderly people

Perks
- A people helping job
- Meet and associate with a lot of people on a regular basis
- See the "world"

Bummers
- You have to be out in all sorts of weather
- Dealing with the public is often difficult
- These jobs are cut back periodically due to budget cuts

Horse's Mouth

Stan Anderson, an actor: "Some of the folks you meet are so appreciative just that you're there. Especially the people in the nursing homes. You get the feeling they'd like it just fine if you spent the whole day with them. Doing any kind of work where you're so appreciated is really rewarding."

Contact

Go to your local library and ask for bookmobile information. Most communities offer these services.

Braille Word Processor

Low Down
In this type of work you create books for the blind. You must learn how to use a specific word processor that turns words into Braille.

Scratch
$15-$25 an hour.

Be
- Able to work on a word processor
- Able to read Braille

Perks
- Many actors do regular word processing; in this type of work, you have the added pleasure of helping the visually impaired
- Usually you can create your own work schedule

Bummers
- As with regular word processing this can be boring, tedious work
- Must learn Braille
- Most Braille word processing companies are not in New York or Los Angeles

Horse's Mouth
Jeri Sesler, an actress: "I was working in a small theater company in Boston when I did this work. The theater didn't pay enough to live on so I did Braille word processing for a few hours a day. There is something nice about knowing your work is helping people."

Contact
- National Braille Press, 88 St. Stephen Street, Boston, MA 02115
- Transformation Inc., 3132 SE J Street, Stuart, FL 33494
- Assoc. Services for the Blind, 919 Walnut Street, Philadelphia, PA 19107

Building Custodian (Janitor)

Low Down

Janitors keep apartment houses, office buildings, stores, hospitals and other types of buildings in good working condition. The smaller the establishment, the more feasible as a part-time job for an actor. (If you accept a job with a large building it's generally full time.) Some actors take the janitor's job in their apartment houses in return for a free-rent apartment. The janitor does everything from fixing a leaky faucet to emptying trash cans to painting to checking the heating and air conditioning.

Scratch

Varies depending on the type of building. Generally from $8-$12 an hour.

Be
- Able to do everything in building maintenance from mopping to repairing
- Comfortable using all types of equipment and cleaning material
- Physically strong
- Willing to work alone

Perks
- Flexible hours on the right jobs (janitors work different shifts)
- A lot of this work available
- Not confined to an office desk
- Not difficult for the person who enjoys physical labor

Bummers
- Constant cuts and injuries
- Some janitorial equipment is very noisy
- Many of the tasks are unpleasant and dirty
- You're on your feet a lot
- Tiring work

Horse's Mouth

Craig Hamilton, an actor: "I am presently the janitor for the building I live in. In payment for my daily chores I receive free rent. When I do extra things for tenants I usually get tipped. Aside from that extra money the building gives me other money when I do special projects for the building (painting apartments, things like that). If I have an audition or a job, my wife or older son usually can take over for a while. It always seems to work out. We live in a small brownstone (nine units) and the work is not usually that demanding."

Contact

The Actors Equity Work Program usually places bulletins up for this type of work. Also check the SAG work board. Another source is the Building Service Contractors Assoc. International, 10201 Lee Highway, Suite 225, Fairfax, VA 22030.

Campaign Worker

Low Down

Obviously this type of work exists when there is an election campaign going on. You'd be surprised though. Aside from national and state political campaigns there are some industries (and large companies) that hold elections and hire a few people to help with their campaigning. It is not necessary that you agree with a candidate's political views so long as you appear enthusiastic about them. The work involves telephoning, filing, leaflet distribution and office paperwork.

Scratch

Varies, but generally $10-$15 an hour or $75 a day.

Be

- Possessed of general office skills
- Comfortable on the phone for long periods of time
- Able to create enthusiasm about candidate (on the phone or while handing out leaflets)
- A good communicator
- Comfortable working in a noisy, crowded environment

Perks

- Can be an exciting, fun place to work
- Potential to work your way up to a better position
- Short term commitment
- Meet a lot of people
- Opportunity to use your acting skills (especially if you don't believe in the candidate)

Bummers

- Can be pressure-filled
- Sometimes you have to work late into the night
- The working conditions can be difficult (crowded, smoky, noisy rooms)
- Generally these jobs are short-lived

Horse's Mouth

Harvey Weintraub, an actor: "I've always gotten a charge from political campaigns. When I first saw the sign up at the Actors Work Program at Equity I thought this could be fun, and it was! It's a few days of as close to crazy excitement as you can get. Whenever I hear about campaign work I'm the first one there. There's always so much activity going on, so much energy!"

Contact

The Actors Work Program at Actors Equity and the Screen Actors Guild job board usually list campaign employment.

Canvas Sampler

Low Down

This is promotional work. Canvas samplers stand on street corners (and occasionally in malls) and hand out free product samples to people walking by. S.M.S.I. is one of the largest canvas sampling companies in the country. They employ independent contractors in different states to hire day workers (the canvassers) for this type of work.

Scratch

Depends on the location and how quickly you can dispense all of the product. Generally workers are paid $55-$75 a day, but in a good location you can dispense all of the product in just a few hours.

Be
- Friendly and outgoing
- Able to work on your feet
- Willing to take a 2 hour training and orientation session
- Dependable
- A people person

Perks
- In a good location you can be through working in just a few hours and yet are paid for the entire day
- Get to meet a lot of people
- Get free samples of the products for yourself

Bummers
- Must work outdoors, sometimes in extreme weather
- On your feet a lot
- Irate passers-by
- Irregular work
- Must work where and when the client decides

Horse's Mouth

Pauline Morgan, who hires workers for this type of work: "We look for friendly people. We hire actors as well as models all the time. The work really isn't too hard, anyone can do it."

Contact

Pauline Morgan – (tel.) 914-997-6926
Joan Shugles – 212-662-7662

Car Rental Clerk

Low Down

Car rental clerks work for companies that lease cars to the public. When hired, you're expected to know all of the company's policies regarding their cars. On the job you inform the customer of the types of cars available and the daily and weekly rates for rental.

Scratch

Starts at minimum wage. In certain areas where competition for workers is tight, wages may be higher. Some companies pay commissions.

Be
- Happy dealing with the public
- Tactful
- Equipped with good oral and written communication skills
- Computer literate

Perks
- Pleasant working conditions
- Discounts on car rentals
- Flexible hours
- Some benefits are offered to part-timers

Bummers
- On your feet a lot
- Customers can be very difficult
- Low paying
- Confined behind a counter

Horse's Mouth

Bonnie Sirgutz, an actress: "I've been working for Hertz for over three years now. It's the perfect job for me, time wise. I can get to auditions and generally work weekends and nights. When I get a show I take a leave of absence and am always welcomed back when I'm available. And the work couldn't be easier."

Contact

Look up any car rental company in the Yellow Pages. Here are some of the larger ones in New York: Avis, tel. (800) 821-2847 and Hertz, tel. (800) 645-3131. Also contact American Rental Assoc., 1900 19th Street, Moline, IL 61265.

Card Reader
(Fortune-telling)

Low Down
People always want to know what the future holds in store for them. Telling fortunes at parties is a playful way to predict the future. The card reader selects cards from the deck and then interprets them. You tell the person about what's going on in the present as well as what may happen in the future. It's important to let the person know that this isn't deadly serious. Readings should be presented as a game.

Scratch
Varies a great deal. Generally about $100 a party.

Be
- Adept at reading cards – you can acquire this skill from books as well as from other card readers
- A good communicator
- Sensitive to people's desires and needs

Perks
- It's interesting, enjoyable work
- The money can be good (tips)
- You get to meet a lot of people
- You may discover your psychic powers

Bummers
- Not a lot of work in this field
- People may treat you badly if they don't believe you or don't like what they hear
- If you are indeed psychic and see something in someone's cards that's negative you can't reveal it

Horse's Mouth
Joan Jaffe, an actress: "All I can say is it's very rewarding when you tell somebody something about themselves and they say 'That's right! That's absolutely right!' Discovering your psychic power is really fascinating!"

Contact
The best way to get this work is by putting signs up on bulletin boards. Also contact party agents. *New York* magazine lists party specialists that hire card readers.

Carpenter

Low Down

There are many types of jobs that carpenters do. The work varies from the construction of buildings to making bookshelves for someone's apartment. Many actors take jobs in construction because the money is good, especially if they join the union. When working on buildings the carpenter is involved in all aspects of building such as: cutting, fitting and assembling materials; framing walls, and hanging kitchen cabinets. Many actors, to supplement their income, will accept small jobs such as replacing a pane of glass or repairing furniture for quick cash.

Scratch

Varies depending on the type of work involved. Self-employed carpenters get about $17-$20 an hour.

Be
- Adept at fixing, repairing, or building
- Willing to undertake employer training programs (for construction work)
- Able to work outdoors if necessary
- Skilled and proficient with all types of tools

Perks
- Can be self-employed or "hire out"
- Work when you want to
- The money is good

Bummers
- Dangerous work (injuries on the job)
- Private customers and employers who make difficult demands vis-à-vis time and performance (quality)
- Work can be strenuous
- Outdoor work in inclement weather

Horse's Mouth

Alvin Cooperstein, a former actor: "I've been doing carpentry work full time for about three years. I enjoy the work, especially working for small construction companies putting up private homes. There's a real satisfaction you get the day you finish a job. It always seems amazing that that home someone's about to move into was once just some land with nothing on it."

Contact

Look up carpenters in the Yellow Pages and ask if they're hiring. Also, contact:
- Associated Builders and Contractors, Inc., 729 15th Street NW, Washington, DC 20005
- Associated General Contractors of America, Inc., 1957 E Street NW, Washington, DC 20006

Carpet Installer

Low Down
Carpet installers install carpet in homes, restaurants and offices. They measure the floors then cut and fit the carpets to fit the area measured. A great many carpet installers are self-employed. Most carpet installers learn their trade on the job.

Scratch
Carpet installers are either paid by the hour or by the number of yards installed. Another consideration is whether the installer is union or non-union. Union installers get $18-$38 an hour. Non-union, usually paid by the yard, get $2-$3.25 a yard.

Be
- Willing to learn this trade through an apprenticeship program (1-2 years, non-union; 3-4 years, union)
- Capable of using such carpet installing tools as carpet knives, power stretchers, knee kickers, etc.
- In good physical condition, capable of bending, stretching, kneeling and lifting
- Able to do measuring and simple arithmetic

Perks
- Flexible hours (work when you want and when a job is available)
- Can set up your own small, part-time business
- The money can be very lucrative
- If working for a company, there is a good chance for advancement to supervisor or instalation manager

Bummers
- Physically demanding
- Injuries on the job (from tools or just the work itself)
- Sometimes you have to deal with irate, dissatisfied customers
- When the economy slows down there is less of this work

Horse's Mouth
Carl Woodbury, an actor: "Presently I freelance with about four companies. I pretty much work when I want to (usually nights and/or weekends). A lot of the guys I work on a job with are actors so this would seem to be 'actor-friendly' work. It can be dull though and some of the big jobs seem endless."

Contact
Look up carpet installing companies in the Yellow Pages. For more information about this type of work contact the United Brotherhood of Carpenters and Joiners of America, 101 Constitution Avenue NW, Washington, DC 20001.

Cashier

Low Down

Cashiers work in department stores, movie theaters, restaurants, supermarkets and anywhere else where there is a need for cash and/or charge payments for merchandise or services. Cashiers receive money, total bills, give receipts and do a host of other chores determined by the establishment and the manager. They are assigned a register and given a drawer each day. Many establishments today utilize scanners and computer terminals.

Scratch

$6 to $13 an hour, depending on the establishment and your experience.

Be
- Very comfortable handling money
- Good with numbers
- Able to use produce scales (in supermarkets) or ticket dispensing machines (theaters)
- Able to do repetitive work accurately
- Neat
- Tactful with the paying public

Perks
- Can lead to head cashier or further
- Flexible hours
- Easy work

Bummers
- Easy to make mistakes
- Boring, tedious and repetitious
- Irate customers

Horse's Mouth

Ray Forson, an actor: "For more summers than I can remember I was a cashier at the Jersey shore. I worked as a cashier in restaurants, movies and shops. If I had an audition there was always someone to cover for me. It's pleasant work, almost mindless, and you get to meet some great people. At least I did."

Contact

The best way to find cashier work is just by walking in and asking. There's a big turnover in this field so opportunities abound.

Cat Sitter (House Sitter)

Low Down

Cat Sitters take care of a client's cats while they're out of town. Some cat sitters also walk dogs, feed fish, whatever. They feed the animals, spend some time with them (cats and dogs), change kitty litter, administer any needed medications and do any other chores related to the animal that the owners request. House sitters take care of apartments or homes while the owners are out of town. They collect mail, sometimes do light cleaning, occasionally answer phone messages and do whatever else they agreed to do for the client. Many house sitters live in the owner's home while they're away.

Scratch

Varies widely, depends on the agreements. Cat sitters generally get $10-$20 a day. House sitters can get $10-$30 a day.

Be
• Responsible
• Dependable
• A lover of animals (catsitter)

Perks
• If you build up a clientele the work can be lucrative
• House sitters get to live rent free in some beautiful homes
• If you like animals, cat-sitting is fun
• Flexible hours

Bummers
• Sometimes the animals are difficult to care for (mean spirited, difficult to give them medication, etc.)
• Have to walk dogs in bad weather
• Losing keys to a client's apartment can be a nightmare
• Animals can get sick when the owner is away and you have to handle all emergencies

Horse's Mouth

Lenore Caveretti, an actress: "Of all the jobs I've had, I enjoy cat-sitting the most. I love animals and taking care of other people's animals is a dream. For the most part the animals are always loving and affectionate and the work itself couldn't be easier. I've built up a clientele and I'm always busy. During the Christmas holidays you can really do very well."

Contact

This is self-starter kind of work. Put up signs on bulletin boards, place ads in your local newspaper and tell everyone you know.

Census Taker

Low Down

Census takers canvass door-to-door in specific neighborhoods to interview the residents. This information is then reported to a government agency (usually the employer). Questions are specific and concise so that the census taker can do the job in the resident's doorway in just a few moments.

Scratch

Varies, generally $200-$300 per week.

Be
- Organized
- Able to coax people into talking
- Friendly and outgoing
- Equipped with good "people skills"
- Persistent
- A bachelor's degree recipient (in some cases)

Perks
- Generally you make your own schedule – you can make an audition and then return to the area you're canvassing
- Exercise and fresh air
- In inclement weather you're not obligated to canvass, instead you work at the office doing paperwork and setting up schedules

Bummers
- People are often rude
- You have to deal with government bureaucrats
- On your feet a lot

Horse's Mouth

Michael Cannis, an actor: "Personally I like the freedom this work gives me. I make up my own schedule. I also like to meet so many different types of people."

Contact

The Actors Work Program occasionally has information about government recruiting for census takers. You can contact the National Institute of Health for information about their next census hiring schedule.

Civics Instructor

Low Down

Civics instructors work for immigrant service organizations and provide classroom instruction to adult immigrants preparing for their US citizenship examinations. The instructor's responsibilities include delivering a pre-developed curriculum on US history and civics and attending orientation and program meetings. The program is held for 11 consecutive weeks (usually Tuesdays and Thursdays, 10 AM to 12 PM).

Scratch

Depends on experience and qualifications.

Be

• Patient
• A bachelor's degree recipient
• Able to work independently
• Experienced in civic training
• A people person
• A good communicator

Perks

• Very rewarding work (patriotic)
• Commitment is only a couple of hours a day
• Meet all kinds of people from all over the world
• You get to use many of your acting skills

Bummers

• Work can be very frustrating
• Students can be difficult
• Not ongoing work
• Generally the money is not that good (but you are only working a couple hours a day)

Horse's Mouth

Reginald Mandofa, an actor: "I have enjoyed this work immensely. It's not about the money, believe me. If you're trying to make a lot of money, this isn't the job for you. The pleasure you get when your people pass the exam (US citizenship) and are so grateful to you, there are no words to express how wonderful that feels. No words, believe me."

Contact

Ms. Debra Cloud-Marcus, Human Resources Department, New York Assoc. for New Americans, Inc., 17 Battery Place, 7 South, New York, NY 10004-1102. For more information call (212) 425-2900, extension 3643.

Coat Check Attendant

Low Down

A coat check attendant takes coats and bags from guests at parties, restaurants or events. They generally are assigned a coat check room where the guests bring them the items to be checked. They are responsible for making sure that the guest gets an identifying tag. At the end of the evening the guest returns the tag to the attendant and receives the coat or bag back.

Scratch

Varies, depending on the arrangement with the restaurant or catering company. Many restaurants pay minimum wage and tips are most of the money. In other restaurants the establishment splits the coat check tips. Caterers pay $10-$20 an hour to coat check attendants since tipping is less frequent at events.

Be
• Organized
• Polite and professional
• Dressed appropriately (a tux for catering work)
• Able to get coats and bags quickly and efficiently
• Friendly

Perks
• Can be good money
• Flexible hours (for caterers you work when you want; restaurants are generally actor-friendly)
• Meet all types of people

Bummers
• Work can be physically demanding (heavy winter coats)
• Irate and rude customers
• On your feet a lot
• Sometimes late hours (you have to wait for all the guests to leave)
• Work can be boring and tedious (slow nights)

Horse's Mouth

Mary Jo Allen, an actress: "Basically it's simple and easy. Also when I get a job my boss always has someone who can cover me, even if I book out of town. When I get back I always have my coat check job waiting for me."

Contact

All catering companies hire coat check attendants, as do most restaurants. One company that hires coat check attendants for special events is ETEMCO, Inc., 150 Broadway, New York, NY 10007; tel. (212) 233-1111.

College Basketball Referee

Low Down

For the actor who's a sports enthusiast, college basketball refereeing may be the part-time job you're looking for. To be eligible for this type of work you must pass the state certification exam. Usually, you have to work your way up to college refereeing, starting with high school or junior varsity. Attending basketball clinics and seminars is helpful. After about five years at the high school level you can apply to the college conference in your area.

Scratch

Varies, generally $175-$375 per game.

Be
• A great basketball fan
• A fair-minded person
• Able to make quick decisions
• In good shape (with excellent eyesight)

Perks
• You are part of a sport you really enjoy
• You experience that adrenaline rush that happens only during live sports
• The work is challenging

Bummers
• To get to NCAA referee status takes a lot of work, more than some actors can give
• Finding a college job can be difficult
• There can be scheduling conflicts
• If you want to work you may have to work games out of your conference

Horse's Mouth

Hank Nichols, NCAA national coordinator of men's officiating: "We have doctors, lawyers, firemen, teachers, policemen, businessmen, you name it...A person needs flexibility if he wants to work games outside his conference."

Contact

National Federation of State High School Associations, 11724 Plaza Circle, PO Box 20626, Kansas City, MO 64195.

Computer Consultant

Low Down
Actors who are computer whizzes are finding that computer consulting work is lucrative and compatible with their acting careers. In this type of work you assist customers in purchasing their computers, help with hardware and software upgrades and repairs, and teach the client how to operate their computer and its different programs.

Scratch
From $40 to $150 an hour.

Be
- Well trained in all aspects of computers
- Knowledgeable about the latest hardware and software
- Experienced in computer breakdown problem solving
- Able to communicate computer operation, maintenance and problem solving
- Properly equipped (a good computer tool kit)

Perks
- Interesting, challenging work
- Meet a lot of people
- Recommendations lead to more work
- Excellent money

Bummers
- When you can't figure out what the solution to the problem is
- When the solution to the problem is time-consuming and the customer can't afford it

Horse's Mouth
Les Remsen, an actor: "There are a lot of people out there who are ill-prepared to do this sort of work. You really have to know what you're doing. People spend thousands of dollars on their computers and need expert advice. Unless you're really up on the latest hardware and software and know all types of computers, I advise you to avoid this work. Customers expect you to know everything."

Contact
This is self-starter kind of work. Put signs on bulletin boards and ads in local newspapers. Most of this work comes through recommendations. If you're good, your customers will pass the word on.

Cook

Low Down
Cooks work privately, for restaurants, catering companies, and institutions. The short-order cook works in fast-service restaurants and coffee shops. The specialty-order cook prepares limited selection menus for fast-food restaurants. They prepare certain foods which are prepared to order or kept warm until ready to be served. As the name implies the cook cooks. The size of the kitchen, the utensils, the work demands all vary from job to job and kitchen to kitchen.

Scratch
Varies, depending on the establishment – goes from about $8 an hour on up.

Be
- Familiar with all types of food preparation
- Familiar with many types of menus
- Well organized
- Able to work as part of a kitchen team
- Personally clean

Perks
- The satisfaction of creating a meal that pleases people
- The creativity of cooking
- Private or catering work can be scheduled at your pleasure

Bummers
- Kitchen accidents
- Customers not pleased with the taste of the food you cooked
- Working in a hot kitchen with limited space

Horse's Mouth
Vivian Chavoistie, an actress who works for catering companies: "When you've made a meal that satisfies people it's a really nice feeling. I prefer small dinner parties; they're more manageable. It's always exciting to visit people's homes, see how they live, and work in a new kitchen. I'm lucky that I can afford to cook when I wish and pursue my acting career the rest of the time. I find these careers to be very compatible."

Contact
Look for catering companies in the Yellow Pages. They are always hiring. You may have to begin as an apprentice.
- If you're interested in culinary work contact American Culinary Federation, PO Box 3466, St. Augustine, FL 32085
- For restaurants and hotels: Council on Hotel, Restaurant, and Institutional Education, 1200 17th Street NW, Washington, DC 20036-3097

Cosmetologist and Barber

Low Down

Actors often do this type of work at home on a freelance basis. Some actors supplement their income by working evenings or weekends in unisex hair salons. Barbers cut, style and shampoo hair. A "hairstylist," in theory, usually gives a client more personalized time. The stylist sets hairpieces, gives scalp treatments and provides other services such as facial massages and shaves. The cosmetologist also cuts and styles hair. But they also advise their customers about hair care. They give perms, straighten hair, lighten or darken hair, give manicures, provide make-up analysis and advice, and clean and style wigs.

Scratch

Varies widely if you work alone out of your home. The money in salons ranges from $8 to $20 an hour.

Be
- Equipped with excellent taste and an awareness of the latest hair trends and fashions
- Dexterous
- A state-licensed barber or cosmetologist (for salon work)
- Sensitive to your customer's taste and needs regarding their hair style

Perks
- Creative work
- Can be done at home
- Flexible schedule
- There is always a lot of work available

Bummers
- On your feet a lot
- Customers who are demanding or never satisfied
- Constant exposure to chemicals (for hair and nails)
- Working for temperamental bosses

Horse's Mouth

Eileen Scarpone, an actress: "I've been chopping hair at home for at least ten years. I really love it. I usually work at night (if I'm not in a show) or on weekends. Weekends are really big! For me it's a creative outlet. The tip I get at the end is like applause. It's immediate gratification!"

Contact
- To get the lists of barber shops in your area contact the National Assoc. of Barber Schools, Inc., 304 South 11th Street, Lincoln, NE 68502. Tell them where you live and that you'd like to contact shops in your area.
- For Cosmetology (training schools and licensing requirements): National Accrediting Commission of Cosmetology Arts and Sciences, 1333 H Street NW, Suite 710, Washington, DC 20005.
- Advertising and bulletin boards to start a business at home. If you're good, word of mouth will take care of the rest.

Counter Clerk

Low Down

Counter clerks work everywhere from video stores to dry cleaners to supermarkets. One thing all counter clerks have in common is that they must know what the company's policies and procedures are. They are responsible for answering questions, taking orders and receiving payments. Most counter clerks work with scanners and computer terminals.

Scratch

Usually counter clerks start at minimum wage but can earn three or four times that amount depending on their experience and the length of time at the job.

Be
- A high school grad (usually)
- Capable of learning on the job
- Tactful in dealing with the public
- Neat
- A good communicator

Perks
- A good, bottom level way to learn about a company
- Excellent chance for advancement
- Flexible hours
- You get to meet a lot of people

Bummers
- Irate customers
- Always the risk of robbery
- On your feet a lot
- Usually you're confined to a small working area
- Can be boring

Horse's Mouth

Jean Douglass, an actress: "I guess everyone's worked some counter job somewhere. I worked for years every summer at the dry cleaning store in my neighborhood (nights and weekends). It was pleasant enough work, and you get to know people, but it wasn't brain surgery and the money wasn't so great so eventually I needed to find a better paying part-time job."

Contact

The best way to get this work is to walk into whatever store you'd like to work in and ask if they're hiring. Some stores put signs in their windows. Another way: Equity and SAG put up notices of employees looking for help. Also try contacting the American Rental Assoc., 1900 19th Street, Moline, IL 61265.

Croupier

Low Down

The actors I spoke with work as croupiers primarily during the summer at Atlantic City. To be a croupier you must be trained in such "primary" games as blackjack and craps, and "secondary" games as roulette and baccarat. You must develop what's called a "good smooth deal." One basic requirement to becoming a croupier in New Jersey is to fill out a 22-page application for the New Jersey Casino Control Commission. Your background will be thoroughly checked. Dealers work nine to ten hour shifts with a 20-minute break every hour. Casinos always have jobs for good croupiers.

Scratch

Varies, but generally about $10,000-$20,000 a year for part-time work (includes tips).

Be
- Quick with your hands and eyes
- Able to develop a smooth dealer technique
- Able to concentrate

Perks
- There is always work
- The money is good
- Work when you're available

Bummers
- The work is tedious
- You have to deal with drunks and/or bad losers
- Smoke-filled, noisy casinos

Horse's Mouth

Josh Fixon, an actor: "I grew up in Jersey and after college did croupier work in the summers. Once I started auditioning in New York I just kept my contacts in the casinos and continued working summers in Atlantic City. It's not a hard job and the money can be good. You get to know a lot of the people who work in the casinos. There's a lot of regulars who come back summer after summer."

Contact

To work in Atlantic City you have to attend a state-approved school. Here's a couple you can look into:
- Atlantic Community College Casino Career Institute, 1535 Bacharach Boulevard, Atlantic City, NJ 08401
- Casino Schools, Inc., 1823 Bacharach Boulevard, Atlantic City, NJ 08401

Customer Representative

Low Down

The company representative deals with all incoming inquiries regarding the company's policies, merchandise or services. This is not a telemarketing job. You represent the company and are expected to handle all inquiries efficiently with intelligence and courtesy.

Scratch

Generally starts at about $8 an hour.

Be
- Computer literate
- Comfortable on the phone
- Tactful, friendly and professional
- Available to be trained for the job

Perks
- Flexible schedules
- Chance for advancement

Bummers
- Difficult customers
- Hard on the vocal chords
- Confined to a desk and a phone
- Not always easy to find this kind of work on a part-time basis

Horse's Mouth

Alana Scwendell, an actress: "I was a customer representative for a couple of weeks and found it to be a difficult job. If you don't mind people complaining and even yelling then maybe it's a job for you. I just couldn't listen to one more kvetch. A lot of people ask to speak to a customer representative, but they really want a complaint department (which not too many companies have)."

Contact

Most companies hire customer representatives. Check the Actors Work Program to see when jobs come up. One company that has hired customer representatives in the past is Wall Street By Fax, 650 Madison Avenue, New York, NY 10022; tel. (800) 659-0555.

Deckhand On A Schooner (Or Other Tall-Masted Sailing Ship)

Low Down

For the actor who loves boats, the ocean and adventure this is the perfect part-time job. Here on the East Coast alone there are over 20 sailing vessels that provide ocean vacations. Some small boat experience is a prerequisite for this type of work. Shops such as The Mystic Clipper and the Spirit of Massachusetts continuously hire part-time employees.

Scratch

About $125 a week (plus room and board).

Be
- Able to work 10 to 12 hours a day
- Comfortable at sea
- Knowledgeable about how to sail a large ship
- Capable of coping with tough ship masters

Perks
- Ocean travel and adventure
- Meet people from all over the world
- Work when available

Bummers
- Danger of drowning
- Bad weather is rough
- Menial work (such as cleaning the toilets)
- Demanding, exhausting work
- Ship captains are demanding

Horse's Mouth

Alan Dagnon, an actor: "I have only wonderful memories of working on a schooner—I met my wife on one. At times the work can get a little crazy, but by and large it's the last of the great adventures. I think it's why all those books and movies were written about the sea. We still go out on vessels together, I just don't work them anymore."

Contact

American Sail Training Association, Newport Harbor Center, 365 Thames Street, Newport, RI 02840.

Dispatcher

Low Down

Dispatchers work for the police, ambulance and fire departments. They also work for trucking, taxi and gas and water companies. Basically, they receive and transmit calls and coordinate them with the appropriate service provider. Their job is to see that the service is provided quickly and accurately. They keep records of all calls and the action that they took. In some cases lives are literally in their hands.

Scratch

Wide range depending on the organization and the location. $6 to $17 an hour.

Be
• Able to think quickly
• Well organized
• An excellent communicator
• Able to calm people in an emergency
• Level headed
• Computer literate

Perks
• Rewarding work – in some cases you save lives
• Flexible hours – this is round the clock work
• There are a great many part-time job opportunities in this field

Bummers
• Work is very stressful
• Seated most of the time (neck and back problems)
• Constantly using your voice

Horse's Mouth

Elaine Steiner, an actress: "I worked as a dispatcher for a tow truck company for about three years. And there were nights, believe me, you want to talk about drama...? The work goes from dull, dull, dull, to crazy and very scary."

Contact

If you'd like some more information about fire, police and emergency services: Associated Public Safety Communication Officers, 2040 South Ridgewood, South Daytona, FL 32119. For more information on other dispatchers: Communication Workers of America, 1925 K Street NW, Washington, DC 20006. Also contact your local police and fire department personnel office for part-time job opportunities in this field.

File Clerk

Low Down

File clerks receive, classify, update and store information for a company. Part of their job is to code incoming material in alphabetical order, by number or by subject. The file clerk stores all pertinent receipts and correspondence. They are also responsible for destroying outdated material.

Scratch

Varies widely.

Be
- Organized
- Adept at all secretarial skills
- Comfortable working in an office
- Able to do repetitive work

Perks
- Good chance for advancement
- Many companies like to hire actors on a part-time basis
- Always work around

Bummers
- Work is often boring and tedious
- The office environment is not for all actors
- Little creative outlet here
- Management can be very demanding

Horse's Mouth

Helen Steiner, an actress: "I do temp file clerk work to pay the bills. What can I say? It's not the most exciting work, but it helps pay the bills. You work when you're available, and sometimes you work in friendly offices with people who are in 'awe' of actors!"

Contact

Look up temp agencies in the Yellow Pages or look for their ads in *Backstage*.

Flea Market Operator

Low Down

Actors are increasingly earning extra income by selling such things as crafts, clothing, furniture and antiques at weekend flea markets. Booths generally cost between $25 and $100 per day and can bring in hundreds of dollars every week.

Scratch

Varies widely. It depends on whether you're working a small neighborhood flea market or a huge parking lot flea market. Also it changes with the item you're selling and how "hot" that merchandise is at that particular flea market. Weather is an important factor. A booth should gross at least $100 a day.

Be
- A good salesman
- Knowledgeable about what merchandise sells best at which flea markets
- Able to be on your feet up to 12 hours in one day
- Friendly and able to bargain

Perks
- You meet all kinds of people
- Get to be outdoors in nice weather
- If you have a good location and desirable merchandise the money can be very good
- It's your own business
- Flexible schedule

Bummers
- Difficult customers
- Slow sales
- Inclement weather (in outdoor flea markets)
- Theft
- A bad location can be deadly

Horse's Mouth

Dwayne Harrelson, an actor: "I've worked flea markets for years (even before coming to New York). Not only is the money usually good, you get to meet some of the greatest people. It's a social thing too. The atmosphere is friendly and I don't know, it's just a great way to spend a Sunday."

Contact

Find out where the flea markets are in your area. Scout them out. See what locations are best, how much the booths cost, what merchandise is selling and how many people go through on a typical day.

Flight Attendant

Low Down

Flight attendants look after passengers' needs on airplanes. They make sure that passengers are comfortable and safe. Part of the job is to prepare and serve food and beverages. Flight attendants must be certain that all emergency equipment is in good working order, greet passengers, check tickets, assist passengers in storing their luggage and instruct passengers in the use of emergency equipment. When the plane is airborne their job is to make the passengers comfortable. Because of the nature of flight scheduling, many actors find that they can do this type of work and still maintain an acting career.

Scratch

Beginning flight attendants earn $15,000 a year (plus extra money for overtime and night and international flights). They get reduced fares for themselves and their immediate families. With six years of experience they earn about $23,000.

Be
• Poised and resourceful
• Comfortable working with all types of people
• In excellent health
• A high school grad
• Willing to take four to six weeks of training for this work
• Able to speak clearly

Perks
• Great travel benefits
• You meet people from all over the world
• Usually have at least 11 or more days off a month

Bummers
• Rough flights are unpleasant
• Standing most of the time
• You must always be pleasant and courteous even with the most obnoxious
     passengers

Horse's Mouth

Yvonne Morris, an actress: "I've been a stewardess for about 12 years. I've managed to keep my acting career alive and still fly. I've loved traveling since childhood and obviously I couldn't find a better job. I think I've been just about everywhere. It's also an escape from some of the pressures of acting; you know, the rejection and all that."

Contact

To get the addresses of specific airlines and to find out more about work in this field contact Future Aviation Professionals of America, 4959 Massachusetts Boulevard, Atlanta, GA 30337 or call toll free (800) JET-JOBS.

Flyer and Brochure Distributor

Low Down
Bulletin boards are located in supermarkets, stores, community centers and some apartment buildings. They represent an inexpensive and effective way to get a message to a lot of people. A flyer and brochure distributor is hired to affix notices to the many bulletin boards throughout the city. It is the distributor's responsibility to locate the "hottest" bulletin boards.

Scratch
About $60 to $75 per client per notice (covers up to 100 locations).

Be
- Aware of the locations of the best bulletin boards
- Mobile (have a bicycle or be willing to walk to all locations)
- Willing to work in all kinds of weather
- Able to convince prospective client that this service will do the job

Perks
- Pleasant work
- If you build up a clientele the money is good
- No pressure

Bummers
- Work in inclement weather
- Your notices are quickly covered by another person after you leave
- Not easy to build up a clientele

Horse's Mouth
Johnny Ammington, actor: "I've just started doing this kind of work. With only six or seven customers, making the trek each week hardly seems worth it. Eventually I'm hoping to build up to 20 or 30 regulars. At the beginning you first have to scour the city and find the best bulletin boards. Those that are overcrowded are not worth bothering with. Once you jot down all the locations you have to work out the quickest route. It's not really difficult, just initially time consuming."

Contact
This is really self-starter kind of work. Post your own ads on bulletin boards everywhere and place ads in local papers. You can also contact businesses and try to sell them.

Food Stylist

Low Down
The food stylist's job is to make food look great in food-related magazines, or for TV commercials or print ads. It's the stylist's job to make that burger look "mouth watering" and that salad "picture perfect." This actor-friendly work is a good networking opportunity. The way to start out is by assisting other stylists on a shoot. Eventually you'll develop your own style and reputation.

Scratch
Varies, but generally $350-$450 a day

Be
- Comfortable handling and working with all types of foods
- A person with a strong "visual sense"
- Knowledgeable about photography (both in front of and behind the camera)
- A good cook

Perks
- You work when you're available
- A good source for networking for other work
- Feeling of accomplishment when your display is attractive and well received
- Nice money
- Can be a lucrative second profession

Bummers
- Sometimes you have to travel out of state to locations
- To "pay your dues" you have to assist established stylists who may be demanding and not pay very well
- There is always the possibility of food damage on a set; food that gets burnt while cooking or discolored so badly it can't be used
- There is a lot of pressure on a TV commercial or print set

Horse's Mouth
Joseph Easwold, an actor: "I've assisted on a few TV commercials as a food stylist. It's a lot more creative than you'd think. It's amazing what can be done. Everything from how the food is cut to the way it's displayed and shot is worked out in minute detail. I find the work interesting and challenging."

Contact
The best way to get started in this work is to buy a copy of the *Creative Blackboard*. This book tells you what's going on in the advertising industry.

Foreign Language Teacher

Low Down
The foreign language teacher works either on a one-to-one basis or in small groups (no more than five students). He (she) teaches all aspects of the language from grammar to conversation. The more languages the teacher can speak fluently the better the opportunities. He should be adept at teaching both beginners and advanced students.

Scratch
From $30-$80 an hour, varies between individuals and groups.

Be
- Fluent in the language that you're teaching
- An excellent communicator
- Patient
- Sensitive to your students' frustrations
- Able to adapt to your students' schedules

Perks
- The money is good
- Very rewarding to see students master a language
- Meet interesting people and work closely with them
- Make your own hours
- Keep up your second language(s)

Bummers
- Students who cancel at the last minute
- Bounced checks
- Frustrated students who give up

Horse's Mouth
Jean Dassin, an actor: "I love this work almost as much as acting. There is no greater joy than seeing one of your students finally "get it." When they start feeling secure speaking to me in French, the look in their eyes, it's so exciting!"

Contact
Teaching privately is more lucrative than teaching at a school. However, setting up a business is expensive and time consuming. Here are a couple of schools that hire foreign language teachers:
- Berlitz; tel. (212) 765-1000
- Language Center; tel. (212) 454-4074

Freelance Fund-raiser

Low Down

A freelance fund-raiser assists in raising money for benefits and special events. The events can be raffles or benefits or galas depending on the organization you're working with. There's a lot of phone work and letter writing involved in this type of work. Basically what you're doing is getting the initial funding to underwrite the event.

Scratch

$12 to $17 an hour.

Be

- Good on the phone
- Able to convince people that the cause (event) is of major importance
- Computer literate
- Able to make quick decisions
- Ambitious and energetic

Perks

- See an event actually take place as a result of your hard work
- Meet a lot of people
- Good networking
- Work only the events you want to
- Fulfilling to help charities you believe in

Bummers

- It is difficult to raise money
- Pressure-filled work
- Bosses can be difficult
- Events can fail, not work out, be poorly attended

Horse's Mouth

Tarryn Quinn, an actress: "I realized a lot about my strengths doing this kind of work. I developed strong skills for dealing with people. But there was nothing quite as rewarding as seeing an event take off, especially when it was a cause that I believed in."

Contact

There are many fundraising organizations that hire people on a freelance basis. Look them up in the Yellow Pages under fundraising counselors and organizations. One that I've heard good reports about: American Assoc. of Fund-Raising Counsel, Inc., 25 West 43rd Street, New York, NY 10036; tel. (212) 354-5799.

Gardener

Low Down

Gardeners help maintain lawns, plant flowers and vegetables, and sometimes help design lawns. The main function is to keep the lawn healthy and free from weeds. They do this by feeding, watering and pruning the lawn on an ongoing basis. Gardeners work for estates, homeowners and in public gardens. Groundskeepers work for golf courses, cemeteries and on athletic fields and generally have more varied duties.

Scratch

Varies between $8 and $15 an hour (lower at the beginning).

Be
- Comfortable working outdoors
- Knowledgeable about pesticides, insecticides, power lawn mowers, chain saws, pruning saws, rakes, shovels, snow blowers, electric clippers and other simple garden equipment
- Able to do your work in a neat, orderly fashion
- Blessed with a green thumb

Perks
- Results of this work can be very satisfying
- There is always a lot of work
- Quite often you can schedule this work at your convenience

Bummers
- Have to work outdoors in all kinds of weather
- Injuries from equipment
- Difficult to satisfy customers
- Illnesses and reactions to insecticides and chemicals
- Physically demanding work
- Wages are low for beginners

Horse's Mouth

Ronald Stern, an actor: "I find this kind of work very complementary to my acting career. It's creative and I work when I'm available. I've developed some regular customers whose gardens I tend on a regular basis with the brunt of the work being done on weekends."

Contact

Professional Grounds Management Society, 10402 Ridgland Road, Suite 4, Cockeysville, MD 21030. Look up gardening companies in your Yellow Pages. There is always a need for apprentice help (a good way to learn this work).

Greeter
(For Hotel Dining Rooms
and Restaurants)

Low Down
Greeters greet customers as they arrive in the dining room. Part of their job is to seat customers and also take phone reservations. They are generally the first person a diner sees when he enters the establishment so their appearance and demeanor are very important.

Scratch
Generally from about $10-$13 an hour

Be
• Neat looking and well groomed
• Friendly, polite and professional
• Well organized
• Comfortable on the phone taking reservations

Perks
• Many establishments are actor-friendly (flexible hours)
• Not a very demanding job
• Shifts are generally only four to six hours

Bummers
• Customers can be difficult and demanding
• On your feet a lot
• Your clothes must be constantly laundered and dry-cleaned

Horse's Mouth
Helen Shapiro, an actress: "I've worked in several restaurants in New York as a greeter. I find the work easy and pleasant. For a woman my age it's the perfect part-time job to go along with an acting career. I can still have a life and earn nice money. Depending on the restaurant, there can be some very nice tips."

Contact
Check the Actors Work Program at Actors Equity and the SAG board for this work. One hotel that hires greeters for their restaurant (Restaurant Charlotte) is the Hotel Macklowe, 145 West 44th Street, New York, NY 10036; tel. (212) 768-4400.

Hand Model

Low Down

This is work where only your hands are seen. The work may be television, film or print. You hold or display a product and/or are the hands of a principal actor in a film.

Scratch

$250 an hour for print (but can be negotiated); $366.25 for film (SAG); $243.60 for tape (AFTRA).

Be
- Able to work in tight spaces
- Physically dexterous
- Possessed of flawless hands
- Able to concentrate for hours
- Able to make small, accurate movements (TV and film)

Perks
- Excellent money
- Generally photographers are friendly and easy to work with
- As you become more successful you can negotiate higher fees

Bummers
- Must maintain your hands in very uncomfortable positions
- Work is limited by how well your hands age
- Must always keep hands out of the sun
- Hands must always be protected

Horse's Mouth

Chris Nelson, one of the top hand models in New York: "Through hand modeling I've learned a great deal about creating a business. There are mailings, developing ongoing business relationships with photographers, clients and art directors. The work itself can be very challenging."

Contact
- Gilla Roos Models; tel. (212) 727-7820
- Parts Models, 500 East 77th Street, New York, NY 10021; tel. (212) 744-6123

Health Club Receptionist

Low Down

The health club receptionist is the first person the customer sees as they check in prior to their workout. The receptionist signs customers in, answers phones, deals with minor complaints and handles most sales and service transactions.

Scratch

$7 to $10 an hour

Be
- Friendly and outgoing
- Responsible
- Patient
- Efficient, able to deal with small details
- Able to make change, handle complaints

Perks
- Free membership at the health club
- Staff discounts
- Meet all kinds of people
- Can be a pleasant place to work

Bummers
- Some clubs are not flexible about work schedules
- Some shifts are quiet and dull
- On your feet a lot
- Irate customers
- Can be stressful at times

Horse's Mouth

Naomi Brisman, an actress: "To do this type of work it's expected that you have a good energy level. No one who's about to work out wants to see a grouch at the front desk. It's like being on stage. Being patient and understanding in the face of angry and irrational members can prove to be a challenging experience for any actor."

Contact

Health clubs are always hiring for this type of work, there's a big turnover. Contact the club you want to work at and fill out an application. One health club that has a large actor membership is the Manhattan Plaza Health Club. They often hire actors to work the front desk; tel. (212) 563-7001.

Host/Hostess for New York Skyride

Low Down
New York Skyride is a big screen flight simulation ride located on the second floor of the Empire State building. There are shows every twenty minutes. Actors are hired in four to eight hour shifts to prepare people for the ride and then assist them through the experience.

Scratch
$10 to $12 an hour.

Be
- Enthusiastic
- Clean cut
- "Theatrical"
- Between the ages of 20 and 30
- Personable
- A person who likes people, all kinds, lots of them
- Bilingual (helpful)

Perks
- Hours very flexible
- Money is good
- Meet all sorts of people
- Actor-friendly employers
- Watching people having a fun time

Bummers
- You are constantly talking (rough on the voice)
- Always on your feet (four to eight hours)
- Work is repetitive
- Working with the public can be difficult

Horse's Mouth
Tracy, who works at Skyride: "We want hosts who enjoy people and can help them have a wonderful time. Skyride is New York's first flight simulation, big screen, thrill ride. We are looking for hosts who are enthusiastic and personable."

Contact
Tracy/Julia at Skyride, Monday-Friday, 10 AM-5 PM; tel. (212) 564-2224.

Hotel (and Motel) Desk Clerk

Low Down

Desk clerks assign rooms to new guests. They also register guests, answer all questions about the hotel and in some cases even collect payments. The first impression guests get of a hotel is from the desk clerk, so it is a very important position at the hotel.

Scratch

Generally starts at about $8 or $9 an hour.

Be
- Friendly and outgoing
- Polite and tactful
- A good communicator
- Professional

Perks
- You meet all types of people
- If you work for a hotel that belongs to a chain there are discounts
- Excellent chance for advancement
- Flexible hours

Bummers
- Guests can be rude
- On your feet a lot
- Employment in this field is subject to cyclical economic swings

Horse's Mouth

Ivy Sue Nemens, an actress: "I enjoy the work. I work at a very nice hotel which makes it easier I guess. Generally the guests are very polite and the people I work with (quite a few are actors) are fun and pleasant to be with. It's not really difficult work and the time flies by."

Contact

The best way to find this work is to check in with the personnel office at the hotel you'd like to work for. Actors Equity and SAG often list job opportunities. The *New York Times* often lists part-time opportunities for desk clerks.

Housepainter

Low Down

Housepainters apply stain, paint, varnish and other finishes to private homes, buildings and other structures. Many actors like this type of work because they can work on a per job basis. Painters must be able to choose the right paint applicator for each job. Many jobs need several types of applicators. Painters must be able to work on scaffolds (when working on tall buildings). There is quite a bit of climbing and bending in this type work. Part of this work includes mixing paints and matching colors and having a knowledge of paint composition and color harmony.

Scratch

The average pay is about $18 an hour (for maintenance painters) and may go down to $13 per hour for production workers in private industry.

Be
- Willing to take an apprenticeship program
- Knowledgeable about color harmony and paint mixing
- Adept at using all the tools involved with this type of work
- Able to read blueprints
- Able to estimate the cost for a job (if you're working privately for a client)
- Comfortable working at heights

Perks
- You can work on a per job basis
- Sense of satisfaction when you complete a job
- You can learn on the job
- Pleasant, enjoyable and somewhat creative work

Bummers
- Must stand for long periods of time
- A lot of climbing and bending
- Much of this work is done with your hands above your head (you need extra stamina)
- Dangerous (fall from scaffolds, ladders)
- Working with hazardous materials

Horse's Mouth

Eli Reandor, an actor: "I've worked for years as a housepainter part time. I was lucky that my uncle had a construction business so I learned on the job. The money's good, you can work when you want, and it's not really hard work."

Contact

Contact painting and decorating contractors in your area. To find out more about this type of work: International Brotherhood of Painters and Allied Trades, 1750 New York Avenue NW, Washington, DC 20006.

Hypnotist

Low Down

Hypnotists help people to overcome fears, improve memory, stop smoking and lose weight. Virtually anyone can be hypnotized. Learning now to hypnotize someone is not difficult. The basics can be learned in a day or two. *Hypnosis Questions and Answers* by Martin Segall answers most questions you may have regarding hypnosis.

Scratch

Varies, but generally $50 an hour and up.

Be
- Comfortable with people
- Confident that you have the ability to relax strangers
- Eager to help people

Perks
- You make your own hours
- Helping people
- With these skills you can develop an act for clubs and ship cruises
- The money is very good
- Learning the basic skills is quick and easy

Bummers
- There are some people (only about three percent) who cannot be hypnotized
- Initial expense for advertising when beginning a practice
- Occasionally you run across neurotics who seek out hypnotists to solve all their emotional problems

Horse's Mouth

Blanche Maywon, a professional hypnotist: "I personally feel that this type of work is only for the sincere person who wants to help others. It shouldn't be just a quick way to make some money. People come to you with plaguing problems as well as for consoling. Sometimes it takes several sessions until you start to see improvement and relief."

Contact

For more information: International Guild of Hypnosis, 410 South Michigan Avenue, Chicago, IL 60605.

Indexer

Low Down

The indexer reads book galleys for a publisher and marks pertinent information. He "indexes" important phrases, words or themes in the text. His notes are then computerized and alphabetized at the end of the book. It usually takes from two to four weeks to index a 300-page book. Most indexers work at home as freelancers.

Scratch

Varies, can be paid a flat rate by the page, by the job, or $15-$25 per hour.

Be
- Someone with an accurate eye for detail
- A person who enjoys reading for long stretches of time
- Able to read fast under pressure – sometimes there are deadlines

Perks
- You can work at home
- Work when you want
- There is plenty of this kind of work

Bummers
- Sometimes there are short deadlines putting the indexer under tremendous pressure
- Eye strain
- Certain books are difficult to understand (and tedious)

Horse's Mouth

Renee Reardon, an actress: "For me, indexing is a part-time job that allows me to be home with my husband and daughter. I'm a quick reader anyway and some of the books are really fascinating. It's like getting a mini-education on subjects you'd never know about. I still can audition and get around. Working at home is always the best thing for my life."

Contact

- The editorial services section in the Yellow Pages
- Send letters of availability to publishers listed in *Literary Market Place* or *The International Directory of Little Magazines and Small Presses*
- Put an ad in *Publishers Weekly*
- Join the American Society of Indexers, 1700 18th Street NW, Washington, DC 20009

Job Developer

Low Down

It is the job developer's responsibility to locate full- and part-time jobs for an employment agency, as well as to maintain and update the company's employer database. In some companies the job developer assists clients with resume writing and conducts interview technique workshops.

Scratch

Varies, $10-$18 an hour.

Be

- Organized
- Experienced with WordPerfect 5.1
- Eager and ambitious
- Able to scout out potential leads
- Comfortable working in an office
- Capable of running workshops

Perks

- Chance for advancement
- Challenging work

Bummers

- Can be frustrating
- Managements are demanding
- Stuck in an office

Horse's Mouth

Arlene Golden, an actress: "I worked as a job developer, part time, in two different companies over a three-year period. Although the work was sometimes very interesting and stimulating, by and large I found it draining. Trying to be an actress and job developer at the same time was sometimes just too much. Maybe I was working too many hours, but when I'd go to auditions I just didn't have much left in me."

Contact

Look in the Yellow Pages under employment agencies. Some of the biggest ones:

- Career Blazers; tel. (212) 719-3232
- Winston (temporary) tel. (212) 687-7890; (permanent) tel. (212) 557-5000

One company that hires job developers is Multitasking Systems of New York, a nonprofit organization which provides training and vocational services to individuals with HIV/AIDS. They are also open to hiring HIV positive actors for this job. They are at 252 Seventh Avenue, 11th Floor, New York, NY 10001. Speak to Alan Huff, Employment Services Manager.

Library Technical Assistant

Low Down

Library technical assistants work at the Performing Arts/Billy Rose Theater Collection at Lincoln Center. Under the supervision of the assistant curator they work primarily at the public service desk and on the telephone assisting researchers. They assist the public with access to non-book and automated reference sources and assist in processing of serials and other non-book materials.

Scratch

$11,203 based on part-time employment.

Be
- Equipped with a bachelor's degree
- Experienced in library research
- Knowledgeable about library automation
- Familiar with personal computers (WordPerfect or Microsoft Word)
- Equipped with strong oral and written communication skills
- Capable of working on a busy public service desk
- Tactful, professional, neat and well organized
- Knowledgeable about current and historical theater and performing arts

Perks
- A theater related job
- Very interesting and challenging work
- Hours are flexible (but Saturdays and evenings are required)

Bummers
- Working with the public is difficult
- Can't get off evenings (to do a show or showcase)

Horse's Mouth

Arnold Mandman, an actor: "I've always been a theater arts history nut. The traditions, historical significance, major events, all of it. There was a time when I was actually thinking of teaching theater arts rather than being an actor. So when this job opportunity came up I jumped at it. I needed extra money and this was like the best of both worlds. I find it challenging and interesting work."

Contact

Send a resume and cover letter to: Human Resources Department, The New York Public Library, 8 West 40th Street, Box KP-LTA, New York, NY 10018.

Lifeguard

Low Down

Lifeguards work at beaches and public and private swimming pools. They are responsible for water safety and work to prevent drownings and accidents. They also give swimming lessons and teach water safety programs.

Scratch

Varies widely, goes from $8.50 to $20 an hour (and higher) plus extra money for teaching and coaching swimmers.

Be
- Competent
- A licensed lifeguard
- Able to pass a physical test of running 50 meters, swimming 500 offshore meters, and then running another 50 meters all in 10 minutes
- Able to deal with all kinds of people
- Able to assert and maintain authority
- Able to act quickly and calmly in an emergency
- In good health (with quick reflexes and excellent eyesight)

Perks
- Nice way to meet people
- Free access to recreation

Bummers
- Can be tedious
- Indoor pools – inhaling chlorine fumes all day
- At the beach – can be in the sun too long
- Bathers can be difficult to control

Horse's Mouth

Larry Ryder, an actor: "I was a lifeguard at Brighton Beach for three summers. The job has a lot of ups and downs. The money can be good, it's great to be at the beach, you get to know some terrific people. On the negative side, it can get really dull, some folks can make you nuts, and there are days you're burning up from the heat."

Contact

Parks and Recreations Department, health clubs, and apartment houses that have pools all hire lifeguards on a part-time basis.

Mail Clerk

Low Down
Mail clerks distribute information, small packages and documents for businesses and governments. They primarily deal with the company's internal mail, sorting and delivering it to the appropriate employee. They also serve as a link between the post office and company personnel, sorting and delivering incoming mail and preparing all outgoing mail. Finally, they receive packages and mailings from delivery services.

Scratch
Varies, depends on the size of the company and the employee's experience. Generally starts at about $7 an hour.

Be
- Well organized
- Able to deal with large amounts of mail on a daily basis
- Able to lift heavy mail bags
- Dependable
- Equipped with good manual dexterity
- Able to work well within a company's bureaucracy

Perks
- Excellent chance to move up
- Have contact with a lot of people during the day
- Flexible hours
- No formal qualifications or training necessary

Bummers
- On your feet a lot
- Can be very noisy place to work (mail handling machines)
- Work can be tiring and physically demanding

Horse's Mouth
Elias White, an actor: "I started off at the mailroom of the company I'm with about five years ago. People were friendly, work wasn't too hard, I could take off for auditions (and an acting job if I got one) and basically it was an easy gig. Within a couple of years I moved up. Now I run the evening and weekend shift in the mailroom. My company's been terrific."

Contact
These jobs are very easy to get. Check with Actors Work Program at Actors Equity and the SAG board. Try any of the mail-order firms, banks, printing and publishing firms, retail stores and any other large firm and I'm sure you'll find some work.

Market Research Group

Low Down

Everyone has an opinion about almost everything. Market research groups pay for opinions—regarding taste or smell or a new movie or product. Groups range from a few people to a few hundred. The group's opinions are evaluated by the producer. This input often determines whether or not a new product will make it to market.

Scratch

Varies, generally from $35 to $85 for a session.

Be

• Articulate about how you feel about things
• Able to participate in group discussions
• Available when the group is to meet

Perks

• Quick, easy money
• Sometimes you're given product samples
• Can be interesting work
• Get to meet a lot of people

Bummers

• Work can be sporadic
• Some groups don't work well together
• Generally they don't like actors to do this work so you must not mention that you are one

Horse's Mouth

Ari Menshum, an actor: "I've always enjoyed this work. You get to meet some great people and sometimes you really make a difference as to whether a new product will make it or not. The only problem is there's not too much of this work and you can't depend on it. It's just a few extra bucks once in a while. It seems like certain times of the year I get the most calls (winter and spring). I register with a lot of bookers for groups so I do okay."

Contact

Check bulletin boards and local papers looking for people to participate in market research groups. Look up market research groups and analysis in the Yellow Pages and call to register. Remember, it's best not to let them know you're an actor.

Massage Therapist

Low Down

Massage therapists help their clients relax their muscles and release tension from their bodies. There are many forms of massage such as deep tissue massage, shiatsu, sports massage and rolfing. Some masseurs (masseuses) utilize only one of these forms, others combine them for their own personalized type of massage. Actors enjoy this type of work because of the one-to-one aspect of the work and the relief and pleasure it gives their clients.

Scratch

Varies, but generally $40 to $75 an hour.

Be
- Well trained in whichever form of massage you choose
- Knowledgeable about human anatomy
- Educated as to the effect of human behavior on body tension
- Licensed

Perks
- Flexibility of hours
- Seeing a client get up after a massage relaxed and smiling
- Money is good

Bummers
- Building up a clientele takes time
- You have to take classes and train to pass the state exam
- Can't do more than 25 massages a week (burnout)
- Health clubs and spas don't split equitably with masseurs

Horse's Mouth

Tarryn Quinn, an actress: "I suppose what I get mostly out of this type of work is helping other people. I'm a former dancer and massage just seemed to come naturally to me. I enjoy seeing people allowing themselves to be vulnerable and trusting me. When you really think about it, what is acting but vulnerability and trust?"

Contact

- You can find out where you can train from: The American Massage Therapy Institute, PO Box 1270, Kingsport, TN 37662.
- To learn rolfing: The Rolf Institute, 302 Pearl Street, Boulder, CO 80306.

Member of a Yacht Crew

Low Down
Working on a yacht crew is a great adventure. These 38 to 45 foot long boats travel the world seeking adventures in every port. On occasion a boat will find itself shorthanded and in need of another crew member, quickly. If you're free, off you go. The more nautical skills you have the better your chance to get this kind of work.

Scratch
Varies, but generally very little; up to about $100 a week (plus room and board).

Be
- An excellent sailor
- Able to deal with all types of people (especially tough skippers)
- Comfortable at sea
- Able to fix engines, navigate, cook, and, of course, sail

Perks
- You see the world
- Flexible schedule, only work when you want (if work is available)
- Once out at sea there are no expenses
- Meet fascinating people

Bummers
- If you're not compatible with the skipper or crew it can be a nightmare
- Money isn't very good
- Unpleasant travelers can be hard to take
- Bad weather can make the trip difficult
- Accidents, collisions at sea – you can drown!

Horse's Mouth
Harvey Milkinson, an actor: "I've been on quite a few yacht crews. It's one of the best summer get-a-ways I know of. For me, getting out on the ocean is the best way to recharge my batteries."

Contact
Taking the US Coast Guard Sailing and Seamanship course can help to get work. It's free! Call (800) 336-2628. Go to marinas, talk to yard workers, dock masters and yacht club members to find employment.

Messenger

Low Down
Messengers deliver mail, packages and documents either internally (within a company) or externally (between companies). They receive instructions and materials from a central office or via a two-way radio. If working for a courier a fee for the delivery is involved. If the deliveries are external the messenger usually drives a car, a van or a bike.

Scratch
Varies widely depending on the type of messenger. If you work within a company the money starts at minimum wage and can go up to $15 an hour. If you work for a courier service quite often you are paid per delivery.

Be
• Fast on your feet (or whatever means of transportation you're taking) – they always want it yesterday!
• Polite, courteous and dependable
• Physically fit
• Able to read well and take instructions
• Well organized
• Licensed to drive (in some cases)

Perks
• Fresh air and exercise
• Working for courier services is lucrative if you hustle
• Communicate with a lot of people every day (company)
• Good chance for advancement (company)
• Companies offer health and other benefit programs

Bummers
• Hard work
• Outdoor work in all kinds of weather
• Dangerous driving a bicycle on city streets
• Pressure to make deliveries quickly
• Angry customers if delivery is late
• Expense of bicycle maintenance (courier)

Horse's Mouth
Seth Halbrook, an actor: "I've worked as a courier for two years. What I like about the work is the constant challenge. I try to top myself, see how many deliveries I can make in a day. I know the fastest routes all over the city. And when you get a package to someone right in the nick of time you should see the look of appreciation on the customer's face and the big tip!"

Contact
Some of the big messenger services that use actors:
• Able Motorized Delivery Service; tel. (212) 687-5515
• Moonlite Courier; tel. (212) 473-2246
• Bullit Courier; tel. (212) 855-5555

Murder Mystery Actor

Low Down

Here's a job where you really get to use your acting skills. You work at hotels, dinner parties and restaurants. You create a character that's part of a murder mystery. Prior to your showing up at one of these establishments you're rehearsed. During the evening a make-believe murder is committed. The guests at the dinner try to figure out "who done it?" Murder mysteries are performed in small restaurants (perhaps 75 guests) and can be as large as those that are performed on the QE-2.

Scratch

Varies, depending on the company. Dinner parties generally pay $50-$150. Cruise ships can pay up to $450 (plus first class accommodations) for five shows during a two-week period.

Be
- Adept at improv
- A quick study
- Quick on your feet
- Able to do accents and dialects (a plus)
- Outgoing and comfortable with crowds

Perks
- You get to meet very interesting people
- Good chance for travel
- A lot of this work around (especially during holidays)
- Delicious food
- A lot of fun

Bummers
- Hecklers and drunks in the crowd
- Uncertainty what each party will be like

Horse's Mouth

- *Laurel Thornby, an actress: "I feel you have to be very confident to do this kind of work. I've found it to be a great way to meet people. It brings me back to the basics of good acting: making believe and pretending."*
- *Melissa Zullo, an actress: "This work gives me enormous experience working with people as well as a great chance to work on improv skills."*
- *Ron Pacie, who runs Murder Mystery, Inc.: "We basically look for 'people-people.' Talent is a major plus in this line of work, but so is friendliness and being outgoing."*

Contact
- Murder Mystery, Inc.; tel. (516) 673-4979
- Hastlefree Mysteries; tel. (212) 563-5572

Paperhanger

Low Down

Paperhangers cover walls and sometimes ceilings with wallpaper. By "sizing" the wall they prepare the surface so that the wallpaper will stick better. They may have to first remove the old wallpaper by steaming or soaking it or applying a solvent. They prepare the pastes necessary for this procedure, then measure, cut and apply the wallpaper.

Scratch

Generally goes from $13 to $20 an hour.

Be
- Able to stand for long periods of time
- Manually dexterous
- In good physical shape
- A good judge of color
- Willing to take an apprentice program

Perks
- Money is good
- Work on jobs when available
- Good chance for advancement to better jobs (estimators, decorators)
- Can establish your own company after a few years

Bummers
- A lot of bending and climbing
- Always chance of injuries from on the job falls (ladders, scaffolds)
- Sometimes work with hazardous materials
- Need a lot of stamina for some jobs

Horse's Mouth

John McInnery, an actor: "I'll do a paper hanging job once or twice a month when I'm available. I work for several companies on a freelance basis. The only bad part about the job is that sometimes you have to keep your arms raised for long stretches and you can get wicked muscle pain. Other than that it's pretty good work."

Contact

Paperhanging apprentices are always in demand. Contact local decorating contractors and tell them you're available. Also: International Brotherhood of Painters and Allied Trades, 1750 New York Avenue NW, Washington, DC 20006.

Patient Advocate

Low Down

The patient advocate is hired to look after patients' rights in hospitals. They are the liaison between the administration, staff and patient. They deal with any complaints that the patient has regarding his stay at the hospital. After a patient has lodged a complaint with the patient advocate, the advocate mediates.

Scratch

$75-$100 per day.

Be
- A good communicator
- A people person
- Compassionate
- Able to deal with a big bureaucracy
- Assertive

Perks
- Helping people in this manner is very rewarding work

Bummers
- This work is not for the squeamish
- The nursing staff sometimes hassles the advocate
- Lots of meetings
- May be called at odd hours

Horse's Mouth

Barbara Stein, an actress: "Patient advocates use communication skills to run interference for sick people in need. It was a very gratifying way for me to both make money and help people."

Contact

Basically there are two ways to get this type of work:
- Contact the individual hospital and see if they can assist you
- There are sometimes ads in the *New York Times*.

Performer's Tax Consultant

Low Down

A performer's tax consultant helps actors, models and dancers with their tax preparation. The consultant should know all the potential deductions a performer can legally take, all possible allowances the performer may have missed and be able to assist in financial record-keeping (in the event of an audit).

Scratch

$150 to $400 per client/tax filing.

Be
- Excellent with figures
- A good people person
- Sensitive to artists' needs
- Patient
- Up-to-date with tax law

Perks
- Meet all kinds of people
- Sometimes get free tickets to shows
- Work is challenging and rewarding
- When working off-season you get to spend more time talking to and getting to know clients

Bummers
- Some clients come ill-prepared to do their taxes
- Extremely high pressured work during the tax season (12 to 16 hours a day)
- The work is mainly seasonal
- At the beginning you must advertise
- Takes awhile to build up a clientele

Horse's Mouth

Lance Gould, an actor: "I make excellent money doing freelance taxes for actors. If you're good and know the little loopholes you can acquire clients for life. Since the work really starts around February and goes through May, it's not too taxing."

Contact

This is self-starter type of work. Put up signs on bulletin boards and place ads in *Backstage*. To get experience you may want to work for the more established firms for a while. The money's not as good but they quite often will train you. Certainly try calling: H and R Block; tel. (212) 799-2134.

Personal Assistant

Low Down
Personal assistants assist homemakers, entrepreneurs, professionals, and the homebound in their homes. They file papers, manage apartments, do household chores, run errands, return telephone messages and do a host of other chores.

Scratch
Generally $10-$15 an hour.

Be
- Good at working with all kinds of people
- Responsible and dependable
- Good in emergencies
- Neat in appearance
- A good listener

Perks
- The satisfaction of helping the elderly or homebound
- This is your own business
- Some clients are very generous (tips and holidays)

Bummers
- Work is unpredictable
- Clients can be demanding and difficult
- Clients die

Horse's Mouth
Steven Drucker, an actor: "I've worked as a personal assistant for seven years. I still work with some of my original clients. One thing I like about what I do is I choose who I want to work with. At this point I hardly ever put signs on bulletin boards anymore. I work through reference and word of mouth. The secret to the work is letting people feel that you're "there for them." A lot of my clients are elderly or ill. They don't need that much, maybe just a quick run to the drugstore. What they really need is a good ear. It's very rewarding work, believe me."

Contact
This is self-starter kind of work. Put up signs on all local bulletin boards. Advertise in local newspapers as well. Let people know you're available.

Personal Trainer

Low Down

Personal trainers help their clients with workouts either at their home, in a gym or in a health club. Working with the client's physical goals in mind, the trainer sets up a program of weight training, aerobics and stretching. A significant part of the trainer's job is motivation and support. Trainers keep records of the client's progress and discuss effective ways to achieve goals.

Scratch

$50 to $100 per hour.

Be

- Certified by ACE (American Council on Exercise) and/or other sports certifying groups
- A good motivator
- A good role model (in good physical shape)
- Knowledgeable about anatomy
- Well trained with all the equipment you'll be using
- An expert on proper form for all the exercises you'll be teaching

Perks

- The money is good
- Guiding clients to their goals is very satisfying
- Motivating others helps you to motivate yourself
- If you work for a health club you use the facilities free
- Success leads to recommendations
- Many people in show business use trainers (can be good networking)

Bummers

- Dead time – when you have large holes of time in your schedule between clients
- Difficult clients
- Clients whose goals exceed their potential
- Clients who don't call to cancel

Horse's Mouth

- Marc Hochstein, a personal trainer: "I like meeting new and exciting people and helping them to physically challenge themselves to attain their personal goals."
- Daphne Gaines, an actress who's a personal trainer: "As an actor it allows me to stay in shape and not be one of the many actors waiting tables in New York."

Contact

Contact the health club you'd like to work for, put up signs on bulletin boards and place ads in local newspapers. One health club that hires actors is Manhattan Plaza Health Club; tel. (212) 563-7001.

Plasterer

Low Down

Plasterers apply plaster to interior walls and ceilings to form fire resistant and generally soundproof surfaces. They also apply plaster veneer over drywall to give it a smooth or textured finish. Some plasterers create ornamental designs in plaster for rooms. More and more plasterers are applying insulation to exteriors of new and old buildings. Plaster walls are having a resurgence.

Scratch

Averages between $17 and $33 per hour (if you belong to the union).

Be
• In good physical condition
• Manually dexterous
• At least 17 years old (to apply for apprenticeship)
• Able to use the tools of the trade (hand powered trowels, power tools, plaster-mixing machines, piston type pumps, straight edges and others)
• Capable of doing complex decorative and ornamental work (molding, wall and ceiling designs)

Perks
• Job opportunities are increasing in this field
• Can be creative work
• The money can be very good
• Can work on a per job basis

Bummers
• Sometimes have to work outdoors on scaffolds (can be dangerous)
• Physically demanding work
• Work is dusty and dirty, irritating to skin, eyes and lungs

Horse's Mouth

Arnold Planter, an actor: "I've done plastering work on a freelance basis for several small contractors. The money's excellent and usually you get to work with the same crew so you get to know each other. The work can get a little tough sometimes but nothing too unbearable."

Contact

The best way to get this work is to contact local plastering contractors and see if you can apprentice with them for a while. Also: International Union of Bricklayers and Allied Craftsman, 815 15th Street NW, Washington, DC 20005.

Playing Superheroes

Low Down

Here's a fun job where you can use some of your acting skills. You dress up as one of several comic strip superheroes, work malls, trade shows, and sometimes even travel (as far as Guam!). The work involves autograph signing, giving out trading cards and making personal appearances.

Scratch

About $150 per day (a lot more if you have to travel internationally).

Be
- In good shape
- Able to work with the public (especially children)
- Convincing as your character
- Able to create entertainment in your role
- Experienced at improv

Perks
- A lot of fun
- The satisfaction of entertaining kids
- A lot of this type of work is available
- Mostly weekend work
- Employers are actor-friendly
- Travel
- Four-hour shifts

Bummers
- Disruptive people in the crowd
- If out of town you may miss auditions
- Have to go on even if you're ill
- Sometimes malls are crowded and noisy
- Uncertainty about what each job will be like

Horse's Mouth

David Sitler, an actor who's done this work for 11 years: "To put it in a nutshell—we're in the smile business. I find this work to be fun and always emotionally rewarding. It's given me the opportunity to travel and do something that I always enjoy."

Contact

Marvel Comics, 387 Park Avenue South, New York, NY 10016 (Attention: Special Events); tel. (212) 696-0808. Also try some of the other comic book companies.

Postal Clerk and Mail Carrier

Low Down

Postal clerks sort mail and serve customers in post offices. Mail carriers deliver the mail. The postal clerk also sells stamps, money orders, weighs packages for postage, and checks to make sure that the customer's package is in good mailing condition. Carriers either deliver the mail by foot or by vehicle. They are also responsible for collecting mail, money for CODs and signed receipts for certified, registered and insured mail. Many actors do this work on a part-time basis.

Scratch

$11.50-$15.50 an hour.

Be
- At least 18 years old
- Able to pass a written exam
- Able to lift packages that weigh up to 70 pounds (deliverers)
- Well coordinated, able to read quickly
- In good physical condition

Perks
- Good chance for advancement
- Flexible hours (around the clock)
- Good working conditions

Bummers
- Can be boring and tedious
- Can be physically demanding
- Irate customers
- Deliverers have to work in inclement weather

Horse's Mouth

John Sullivan, an actor who also delivers mail: "I think the best part of the job is getting to know the people on your route. I've known some of these folks for several years now. Some of them are really very nice people."

Contact

Call or go to your local post office. They will give you more information about the entrance exams and what part-time jobs are available in your area.

Preschool Worker

Low Down

For those actors who love children this can be a wonderful way to earn some extra money. You take care of children who are five years old and younger. Usually you're employed by either day care homes, preschools or day care centers. You're required to oversee all the children's needs.

Scratch

Varies widely depending on your educational background, your experience and what the employer can afford. Generally low paying.

Be
- Enthusiastic
- Trustworthy and responsible
- Comfortable working with young children
- Quick on your feet and able to deal with disruptive children

Perks
- If you like kids this can be a treat
- Flexible scheduling – usually only a half a day's work
- There's a lot of this work around

Bummers
- Disruptive children
- Very responsible work – draining
- Low pay
- Constantly bending, lifting, standing and stooping

Horse's Mouth

Eva Bataglione, an actress: "There are some things that nourish you. For me, working with children is more pleasure than work. Sometimes I watch them and see such freedom, such creativity! All the acting classes in the world can't give you that."

Contact

Look up day care centers in the Yellow Pages. For more information about this type of work: Childcare Employee Project, 6536 Telegraph Avenue, Oakland, CA 64601.

Program Director for Charity Organizations

Low Down
In this type of work you're responsible for expanding and maintaining already existing programs within a charitable organization. People are sought who can recruit other workers, train and supervise volunteers, work with the media and do community outreach.

Scratch
Varies, depending on the charity. Generally about $15 an hour.

Be
- Computer literate
- Responsible
- Well organized
- A leader
- Able to deal with all kinds of people
- A compassionate, concerned person
- Experienced in volunteer management
- Of a humanitarian bent

Perks
- Very positive type of work; helping people
- Meet all types of people
- Work the hours you're available

Bummers
- There is a lot of pressure on these jobs
- Being around sick and dying people isn't for everyone
- Volunteers aren't always dependable and may leave you in the lurch

Horse's Mouth
Nancy Sondag, who hires for Hearts and Voices, an AIDS organization that was created to ease the isolation and suffering of hospitalized AIDS victims by bringing music, care and comfort to them: "No doubt this isn't the kind of work for everyone. We look for people who are dedicated, capable and responsible. Our program directors deal with 100 performers a month so they must be sensitive not only to our clients but also to the many other performers. Currently we have weekly performances at eight health care facilities plus two creative, dramatic workshops and a bimonthly pediatric program. We are constantly looking for new people for our staff (paid as well as volunteer)."

Contact
Many charitable organizations hire staff only on a full-time basis. I suggest you call the charity you'd like to work for and ask if they're taking resumes for program directors (and other jobs). If you'd like to work for Hearts and Voices: Nancy Sondag, Hearts and Voices, Inc., 150 West 80th Street, #7D, New York, NY 10024; tel. (212) 799-4276; fax (212) 799-7932.

Proofreader

Low Down

After they've worked on a document and made corrections, attorneys at law firms submit the original copies (called "the master") to a word processor who keys in the changes and then prints out the work. The proofreader reads the word processor's version and compares it to the attorney's original draft. The proofreader marks all errors, misspellings and form inconsistencies in red pen. He then sends this PC (proofreader's copy) back to the word processor.

Scratch

Those working for temp agencies:
- 9 to 5 workers, $13-$14 per hour
- 5 PM to midnight, $15 to $16 per hour
- Midnight to 8 AM, $17 to $20 per hour
- Freelancers, generally about $18 per hour.

Be
- Equipped with strong reading skills
- Equipped with an eye for detail
- A good self motivator
- Able to concentrate for long stretches of time

Perks
- Flexible hours (big law firms and brokerage houses operate 24 hours a day, 365 days a year)
- Money is above average
- A lot of downtime (comes to about one-third of your paid shift, waiting for word processors to re-do material – can read a book, memorize lines)

Bummers
- Eye strain
- You never have a set schedule
- There is no job security
- Back and shoulder problems

Horse's Mouth

Larry McNichols, an actor: "I suppose what I like best about the work is the flexibility in scheduling. I only work when I want to. I use the downtime on the job to memorize monologues and read new plays. The work itself isn't very difficult."

Contact

Many temp agencies hire proofreaders. One actor-friendly agency is: Accureaders; tel. (212) 228-7944.

Public Opinion
Poll Taker

Low Down
This work is not to be confused with census taking. Here you call people and solicit their opinions about specific subjects. You are given a questionnaire and read the questions exactly as they're written. Then you either mark their answer in the appropriate answer box or write in the correct word.

Scratch
Generally $10 to $15 an hour.

Be
• Comfortable working on the phone for hours
• Equipped with a pleasant speaking voice
• Friendly
• Neat and well organized
• Able to work in a busy office environment

Perks
• Flexible hours
• Free samples of product

Bummers
• A lot of hang-ups
• Rude people
• Shoulder and back problems from sitting for long periods
• Tough on the voice

Horse's Mouth
Cleave Hiller, an actor: "I've worked for several companies that took public opinion polls on their products. Actually it can be quite interesting. It's not quite as dry as it might seem. You get a sense of what some of the people are like out there. It's almost like entering their private worlds for a few minutes."

Contact
The best place to find this work is through bulletin board ads, newspapers and the Actors Work Program and SAG board.

Public Relations Assistant at the Library

Low Down
The New York Library hires people on a part-time basis to assist in their public relations office. The responsibilities of this job include researching and maintaining the Library's computerized database of media contacts and inputting the Library's monthly events calendar.

Scratch
Starts at $10 an hour.

Be
- Bright and creative
- Proficient on a Macintosh computer
- Able to use Quark XPress and FileMaker Pro
- Available a minimum of 15-20 hours a week
- A good writer and editor

Perks
- Exposure to all aspects of media relations and workings of a large nonprofit cultural institution
- Chance for advancement
- Flexible hours

Horse's Mouth
A worker (didn't wish to be identified) at the New York Public Library: "This work is really for someone who can work within the bounds of the Library and is somewhat creative. The work is interesting and somewhat challenging. If you feel you have the necessary skills, please feel free to apply."

Contact
The New York Public Library, Human Resources Department, 8 West 40th Street, 2nd Floor, New York, NY 10018.

Real Estate Agent

Low Down

Many actors take real estate agent certification exams in order to work in this field. Whether it's renting apartments or selling condos or houses, the rewards can be impressive. A real estate agent should have thorough knowledge of the housing market in their area. They are independent sales agents who provide their services to a licensed broker. The broker pays them a commission on their sales.

Scratch

Varies widely. Depends on where you're located, how good a salesman you are, and the state of the economy.

Be
- A licensed real estate agent (you must take the exam)
- A high school grad
- At least 18 years old
- Willing to take at least 30 hours of classroom instruction
- Friendly
- Ambitious and competitive
- Neat

Perks
- Good money
- Get to meet all types of people in this work
- Good chance for advancement in large firms
- Inside track to good rentals

Bummers
- Pays only on a commission basis – dry spells are discouraging
- Some clients don't know what they're looking for
- Some clients are just passing time
- Must work in all kinds of weather
- May have to work odd hours (to meet the client's availability)
- Initial investment of time and money (studying to take the exam and classes)

Horse's Mouth

Vivian Marshall, an actress: "To me this is a dream job. I pretty much work when I'm available, I make good to excellent money, and I meet some lovely people. I find it to be a perfect side profession to acting."

Contact

There are always positions available with real estate companies. Check the Yellow Pages and see the *New York Times*. For more information on this type of work: National Association of Realtors, 875 North Michigan Avenue, Chicago, IL 60611.

Receiving, Traffic and Shipping Clerk

Low Down

All of these jobs deal with the handling and recording of merchandise either being shipped to or shipped from a company. The extent of their specific duties depends on the size of the company. The traffic clerk keeps records of the weight, direction and charges of all incoming and outgoing merchandise. Shipping clerks are basically responsible for the handling and paperwork for outgoing orders of a company. When shipments arrive it is the receiving clerk's job to handle all the necessary paperwork involved. About two out of ten shipping clerks work on a part-time basis.

Scratch
$9 to $17 an hour.

> **Be**
> • Well organized
> • Responsible
> • Able to work with computers
> • Honest
> • Good with mathematics
>
> **Perks**
> • Good chance for advancement
> • Flexible hours (in some companies this is round the clock work)
> • Many job opportunities
>
> **Bummers**
> • Can be boring (repetitious) work
> • Sometimes the working conditions are not so good

Horse's Mouth

Lance Neilson, an actor: "I suppose the best part of the work is I can work when I'm available. The company I work for covers for me if I'm at an audition or get a job. The work itself isn't too great but I'm earning pretty good money because I've been with the company for seven years. I also get excellent benefits."

Contact

The best ways to find this kind of work are through the state employment service and ads in the *New York Times*. Part-time workers are always in demand in this field.

Receptionist

Low Down

The first person a caller sees at a company is the receptionist. It is important that the receptionist give a good first impression. She (he) greets customers, finds out what they need and refers them to the appropriate person. They're also usually responsible for the phone. When they work for a doctor or in a medical office their job includes getting the patient's chart and sending them to the correct waiting room. In beauty salons they set up appointments.

Scratch

About $8 an hour.

Be
• Friendly and professional
• Tactful and polite
• Well groomed
• Computer literate

Perks
• There are always openings
• Flexible, part-time shifts
• Chance for advancement
• You meet a lot of people

Bummers
• Some people are rude
• Bosses can be demanding and difficult
• Seated for long periods of time (back and neck pain)
• On the phone a lot (hard on your voice)

Horse's Mouth

Gloria Marshall, an actress: "I used to work part time (evenings and weekends) in a doctor's office. Aside from getting more colds than usual I did enjoy the job. It wasn't very taxing and the people (especially the doctor) were very pleasant. I suppose if you have to make some extra money, it is as nice a job as you can get."

Contact

Most state employment agencies list the job openings in this field. The *New York Times* (especially the Sunday edition) is chock full of part-time receptionist opportunities.

Recruiter/Executive Search Research

Low Down

If you like to venture out in the corporate world once in a while this may be the job for you. A recruiter locates executives looking for work and helps place them in new jobs. Responsibilities include researching targeted companies, recruiting the executives (via phone), and making recommendations based on interviews and personal judgment.

Scratch,

Varies, depending on ability and experience. Generally $10-$20 an hour.

Be
• Very assertive and tenacious
• Creative
• Adaptable and mature
• Familiar with organizational charts
• Able to use WordPerfect 5.0 on computers
• Equipped with communication skills
• Willing to be coached
• Able to make fair and accurate judgments of potential job candidates
• Comfortable working in an office

Perks
• Get to work with some very exciting and powerful people
• Excellent chance for advancement
• Work can be interesting and very challenging
• Sense of accomplishment when an executive is properly placed and is satisfied

Bummers
• May take awhile until you're properly trained and ready to do this work
• Executives can be difficult to work with
• This work is very stressful and demanding

Horse's Mouth

Alan Keilson, an actor: "I found this work very stimulating, interesting and exciting. There was a period I was even thinking of doing it on a full-time basis. You get to meet and work with some incredible people. I also liked the challenge, what the job's really about. If you're looking for an exciting way to escape from all the show biz nonsense once in a while this is the job."

Contact

Look in the Yellow Pages under executive recruiter companies. One company that has hired actors part time for this work is: Collaghan Assoc., 119 West 57th Street, Suite 1220, New York, NY 10019; tel. (212) 265-9200.

Repo Man

Low Down

If you're looking for an odd job try working as a repo man. You're hired by repossession companies to find and tow cars whose owners are in default.

Scratch

Varies, but generally about $100 a car.

Be
- Able to think quick on your feet
- Willing and able to deal with very angry owners
- Able to work strange hours (mostly night, early mornings)

Perks
- Every job is unique
- Action job
- Work when you're available

Bummers
- Can be dangerous; sometimes the owners can become violent
- Strange hours
- This type of work doesn't lead anywhere

Horse's Mouth

John Fiskin, an actor: "I was a repo man for a company outside Chicago. I was trying to get acting work there and did it on the side. It was crazy. Usually not much happened, not too hard, but one time I almost got my ear shot off. I got a waiter job shortly after that."

Contact

Check the Yellow Pages for the repossession company nearest you. There are plenty of them.

Retail Salesperson

Low Down
Retail salesperson are hired by just about every type of store to assist customers in selecting and purchasing merchandise. You'll be expected to know how to make out sales checks, receive cash or charge payments, open and/or close out the cash register, stock shelves, take inventory, and even prepare displays (in smaller stores).

Scratch
Usually retail salesperson start at minimum wage (or a little above). Some employers offer a small commission on sales.

Be
• Honest
• Happy working with people
• Tactful and patient
• Neat
• Able to communicate clearly

Perks
• You're constantly meeting new people
• Good chance for advancement
• You don't need a formal education
• A great way to develop your persuasive skills
• You usually get store discounts on merchandise
• There is always work

Bummers
• On your feet a lot
• Some stores pressure employers to work holiday seasons and weekends
• The work is repetitive

Horse's Mouth
Nettie Stein, an actress: "Like many actors I work the department stores during the holiday season. It's a good way to make some extra cash and get discounts for my own Christmas shopping. I always like the feeling in the store around the holidays so it's not really a bad gig."

Contact
The personnel office of any store you want to work in. The bigger department stores are always hiring part-time help around the holiday season. Many actors also work part time during the evenings and on weekends.

Sailmaker

Low Down

Sailmakers sew sails for sailboats. They generally work in "sailmaking lofts" found in most major cities that have sailing activity. These lofts are huge spaces where the sails can be laid out, cut and trimmed.

Scratch

Averages between $6-$12 an hour.

Be

- A person with excellent sewing skills
- Knowledgeable about sails and sailboats
- Aware of different anglings and cuts for sails
- Comfortable working for hours doing sewing work

Perks

- There is always work to be found
- Very few hazards to the job
- Not very demanding
- Once you know this work you can do it in any city with sail lofts
- Can eventually lead to setting up your own sail lofts

Bummers

- Not very good money
- Work can be tedious
- Must live in a city where there is sailing activity

Horse's Mouth

Walter Scanlon, who works at Hild Sails in New York: "Most sailmakers learn their craft on the job. A person who sews well can start right away at the machine."

Contact

Look up sailmaker shops in the Yellow Pages.

Security Officer (Guard)

Low Down

Security officers patrol property to protect it from theft, fire or illegal entry. Also known as guards, they protect a company's records, money or equipment. You'll see guards at airports screening passengers for contraband or explosives. Guards are also hired by schools, art galleries, museums, banks, railroads and department stores. They're hired for social affairs, conventions and for sporting events. "Bouncers" are guards hired by discos or bars. Many actors work as guards because of the flexibility of scheduling.

Scratch

Varies. Public utility guards get about $12 an hour, bank guards get about $9 an hour. Some guards are paid minimum wage.

Be
- Without a police record
- Able to pass an oral and written exam
- Mentally alert
- In good health (especially eyesight and hearing)
- Dependable
- Able to deal with emergencies
- Willing to take drug tests and polygraph exams
- Honest

Perks
- There is always work
- Flexible hours
- A good chance for advancement

Bummers
- Outdoor work in inclement weather
- Sometimes you're confined to a small desk
- Generally you work alone (sometimes for long stretches)
- Generally you have to eat on the job (no meal breaks)
- Can be dangerous

Horse's Mouth

Larry Ellington, an actor: "I've worked as a security guard off and on for about three years. It can get really boring sometimes but it's one of the best jobs you can get to work on a monologue. I've worked on lines for a scene or memorized complete monologues in one or two nights. There's a lot of alone time on the job. And if you work the graveyard shift it's very quiet."

Contact

The *New York Times* is filled with security guard work. It's not difficult work to find. There are always companies looking.

Shopper/Spotter

Low Down

Shoppers/spotters locate and buy phony knock-off products that are being sold in stores and on the street. Such products as clothing, garments, watches and toys are made inexpensively and then sold at low prices. To do this type of work you have to use your acting skills and be able to pass as a shopper, an out-of-town customer or a foreign tourist.

Scratch

Usually about $15 an hour.

Be
- Convincing in the role (tourist, foreigner) you are playing
- Quick on your feet
- Comfortable in all areas of the city

Perks
- Use your acting skills
- Interesting, exciting work
- Work when you're available
- Satisfaction of helping to reduce criminal activity in your community

Bummers
- Unpleasant if you're found out
- On your feet a lot

Horse's Mouth

Ellen Dassin, an actress: "I was a shopper/spotter for one summer a few years ago. Aside from feeling like I was doing something worthwhile, I also felt like I was an actress playing an undercover part. I thought it was a gas!"

Contact

There are many security and investigative agencies that hire shoppers/spotters. Look them up in your Yellow Pages. One is Holmes Hi-Tech, New York, 601 West 26th Street, New York, NY 10001; tel. (212) 647-1400.

Sperm Donor (Men Only)

Low Down

This is not the locker room chuckle you may be thinking it is. It's a well paying job that has a concerted commitment attached. "Specimens" are given twice a week for a 45 to 50 week period. For obvious reasons this is all done anonymously. You are expected to take two blood tests a month. Your health is constantly monitored. More and more actors are participating in this relatively easy way to earn cash.

Scratch

$3,000-$5,000 a year.

Be
- 18 to 40 years old
- Intelligent, educated, in good health
- Genetically okay
- Responsible and willing to keep a year's commitment to the program
- Drug free
- Without alcohol problems

Perks
- Excellent money
- Given a free yearly physical
- Free psychological evaluation each month
- The work (giving a specimen) is easy
- You are helping childless couples conceive

Bummers
- 93 percent of all men's sperm does not freeze well (so they cannot participate in this program) – only 7 percent of all men will be eligible
- Serious commitment for one year
- Must abstain from sex for about two days prior to giving a specimen
- Must wait six months before the first fee is paid for this work
- Must be vigilant about your health
- Must curtail alcohol and especially any drug use (this is monitored)
- You never know the ultimate disposition of your sperm

Horse's Mouth

Albert Anouna, who runs the sperm donor program at Bio-Genetics: "The commitment to do this type of work is a very serious one. Many people refuse to sign the contract commitment sheet. These are people's lives we're dealing with and we have to take every precaution. Male infertility in this country is on the rise, we're not quite sure why. More and more people are looking towards clinics such as ours for help. Male donors are desperately needed."

Contact

Dr. Albert Anouna at Bio-Genetics. Tel. (908) 654-8836.

Substitute Schoolteacher

Low Down

Substitute schoolteachers take over for regular teachers. They are supposed to continue teaching what the regular teacher was working on with the students (according to the curriculum). Substitutes are on call on a daily basis. If a call to work conflicts with an audition or acting job, the offer can always be refused without penalty. The substitute should plan to arrive a little early in order to read the teacher's lesson plan for that day.

Scratch

Varies, depending on school district and whether it's a public or private school. Averages about $100 per day.

Be
- Responsible
- Available
- Well organized
- Able to handle a classroom of students
- A good communicator
- Able to deal with problem children
- Knowledgeable about subjects appropriate to the grade levels you'll be subbing for

Perks
- Children are rewarding to work with
- Work when available
- Each day is an adventure
- Short day

Bummers
- Disruptive children
- Children wear you out
- Assignments at some schools are dangerous (students carry weapons)
- You never know what you're walking into each morning
- Students often take advantage of a substitute teacher

Horse's Mouth

Sue Henderson, an actress: "You can learn so much from children, they talk directly from their heart, uncensored. Working with young children can be a lesson in being open, something an actor always needs."

Contact

Go to the Board of Education in your city and ask for the substitute teachers division. If you want to sub for a private school in your area just go to their personnel department. Sue Henderson got her subbing job going to the 92nd Street Y in New York and inquiring about subbing for their nursery school children.

Teacher's Aide

Low Down

The teacher's aide assists the classroom teacher. They supervise students in the school yard, cafeteria, on field trips and in the classroom. The teacher's aide may also tutor students, help grade exams for the teacher, check homework and do other clerical and paperwork.

Scratch

Earnings vary with work experience and qualifications. Generally about $9 an hour.

Be
- At least a high school grad
- Comfortable working with children
- Able to take instructions from the teacher
- Equipped with good oral and written skills
- Able to operate audiovisual equipment

Perks
- Spiritually rewarding
- Good chance for advancement
- Flexible schedule (as long as arrangements are made in advance)

Bummers
- Children are often difficult to supervise
- Personality problems with teacher
- No auditions during your shift
- Budget cuts occasionally eliminate jobs

Horse's Mouth

Celia Laxford, an actress: "I used to be a teacher's aide for an elementary school. I found the work very rewarding. Working with children is so much fun. The teacher was extremely kind to me and we worked very well together. As I got more auditions (and work) I couldn't commit to the job anymore."

Contact

The school superintendents and State Department of Education. Also contact American Federation of Teachers, Organizing Department, 555 New Jersey Avenue NW, Washington, DC 20001.

Teaching English as a Second Language

Low Down

In this type of work you teach non-English-speaking people how to speak English. Each school has its own method. For instance, the N.Y.A.N.A. (New York Association for New Americans) only allows English to be spoken in the classroom and teaches language in the present tense. They teach through repetition. Instructors are expected to be able to teach everything from grammatical English structure to job skills to cultural education.

Scratch

Varies, depending on your experience. Generally $10-25 an hour.

Be
- A good communicator
- Patient
- A people person
- Someone who understands basic grammatic structure
- Able to be firm with your students when necessary
- Quick and attentive in correcting students
- Equipped with a sense of humor

Perks
- Very rewarding work
- Most employers are actor-friendly
- When you teach you learn
- Use many of your acting skills

Bummers
- This work can be very frustrating
- Can sometimes be difficult to do this work along with an acting career (a lot of "take home work" to do)
- The bureaucracies at the schools can sometimes be demanding
- Difficult students

Horse's Mouth

Michael Cannis, an actor: "I must admit that when I did this work I found it very energizing. I tried to add humor to my teaching and the students seemed to enjoy it. It's like doing a 2 and a half hour monologue every day. When you're up there in front of the classroom you're on stage."

Contact

There are many language schools that offer English as a second language, just look them up in the Yellow Pages. To start you off here's the number for the Berlitz School in New York – 212-765-1000 and 425-3866; and the number for the Language Center – 212-435-4074. Another possibility is N.Y.A.N.A. (New York Association for New Americans).

Telemarketer

Low Down

Telemarketers spend most of their working hours on the phone contacting customers for an employer. They either work with a script in hand or memorize a "spiel" for their employer. They pursue consumers by trying to sell a service or product. This field is broad and there are many types of job opportunities. Some telemarketing projects only call for 20 or 30 hours, many are ongoing.

Scratch

Varies, can go from minimum wage to $15 an hour. Some jobs offer commissions.

Be
- Good on the phone
- Possessed of a pleasant and friendly voice
- Ambitious and motivated
- Able to interact constructively with all types of people
- Confident

Perks
- Those working on a commission basis can do very well
- Flexible hours
- There's a lot of this work around
- Telemarketing offices are usually friendly environments
- Chance for advancement

Bummers
- Can have slow nights (no sales)
- Difficult customers (constant hang-ups)
- Some offices are pressure cookers
- Difficult on your voice
- Long hours seated at desks on the phone are rough on your back and shoulders
- Some offices are windowless, small and dirty

Horse's Mouth

Maryanne Lubow, an actress: "I worked for a company that sold cruises (three to seven nights in the Caribbean). We worked on commission. Maybe my timing was right (it was right before Christmas) but I made incredible money! Unfortunately it was only a one-month job. I had a couple of telemarketing jobs after but none came close to that one."

Contact

The Actors Work Program at Actors Equity constantly has this type of work as does the SAG board. Some companies that are actor-friendly:
- Merrill Lynch, 717 Fifth Avenue, New York, NY 10020; tel. (212) 415-7978 (speak to Malka Bernstein)
- Equitable Financial Companies, 120 West 45th Street, New York, NY 10036; tel. (212) 642-3537 (Mondays are best day to call)
- Concepts In Staffing Executive Search, 9 East 37th Street, New York, NY 10016; tel. (212) 725-0300
- Northwestern Mutual Insurance Co., 61 Broadway, Suite 3015, New York, NY 10006; tel. (212) 425-2670

Theater Technical Director

Low Down
With theater budgets constantly being cut, several smaller theaters are now hiring some of their staff on a part-time rather than full-time basis. Technical directors work with the administrative as well as artistic staff of the theater. They plan, schedule and supervise maintenance of the theater space, light and sound shop, and storage areas and equipment. Quite often they purchase and keep inventory of the technical equipment and supplies needed for the theater. They are responsible for the technical management of the theater.

Scratch
Varies widely, depending on the size of the theater, location, and budget. $15 an hour is a fair starting price for a small theater.

Be
- Responsible and technically proficient in all aspects of theater
- Equipped with three to five years technical theater experience
- Proficient in all aspects of theater production and design, including drafting, carpentry, scene painting, electricity and electronics, lighting, stage rigging, sound design, and production management
- Endowed with strong organizational and interpersonal skills
- Able to work in a hectic artistic environment

Perks
- Extremely challenging
- Very creative
- Excellent way to become part of the theater's company
- Money can be very good
- Very good networking opportunity

Bummers
- Pressure-filled job
- Sometimes have to work with difficult artistic staff
- Work can be all encompassing (you may have to put your acting career on the back burner for a while)
- Budget cuts can affect your job security and wages

Horse's Mouth
Elliot McVey, an actor: "After years of doing technical work in summer stock I thought doing a technical director's job couldn't be too difficult. I saw an ad for a technical director at a small off-off Broadway theater. I applied, got it and regretted every minute of it. Every day it seemed there were insurmountable problems. I had to forget about being an actor. After six months I was out of there. It's a very full-time job. I can't imagine what it would be like in a larger house."

Contact
Contact the small off and off-off Broadway theaters to see if they're looking for a part-time staff. Also check *Backstage* and *Variety* for this type of work.

Theater Ticket Order Taker

Low Down

In this job you answer phones and take orders for tickets to shows. You answer any questions regarding the shows, the theaters, locations and other pertinent information. You are also responsible for other office support work.

Scratch

Generally starts at about $8 an hour.

Be
- Comfortable working on the phone
- Polite and tactful
- Well organized

Perks
- Actor-friendly work (flexible hours)
- Quite often free tickets to shows are available
- Advancement possible
- Casual dress code

Bummers
- Confined to a small area
- On the phone a lot, difficult on the voice
- Customers can be indecisive and/or difficult

Horse's Mouth

Renee Dassin, an actress: "I found this work actually a lot of fun. You'd sometimes meet some very nice (and appreciative) people who really loved to talk about theater. The work wasn't difficult. I mean there weren't heavy demands placed on you, so I never felt really pressured."

Contact

Actually there are quite a few companies that hire actors to work the phone selling tickets. Look up ticket sales, entertainment and sports in the Yellow Pages. One company that has been hiring lately is Theater Direct, Inc., 1650 Broadway, Suite 910, New York, NY 10019; tel. (212) 541-8457.

Tile Setter

Low Down
Tile setters apply tiles to floors, walls and ceilings. They generally work indoors. Over the years tile has become a popular building material because it's easy to clean, water resistant and durable. Tile setters work on jobs in shopping malls, lobbies of buildings, tunnels, hospitals and food preparation areas.

Scratch
Averages from $13-$25 an hour.

Be
- Willing to undertake an apprenticeship in order to learn the necessary skills
- In good physical condition
- Manually dexterous
- A high school grad (preferred)

Perks
- Creative work
- Money is good
- Work indoors
- Less hazardous than other construction work

Bummers
- A lot of kneeling, bending and reaching
- Some tools are hazardous
- Work is not as plentiful as other construction work

Horse's Mouth
Harry Hauptman, an actor: "I suppose what I like best about tiling is as compared to other construction work there is more creativity involved. Also, the work's not as exhausting as other construction work. The only problem is there's not too much of this work around."

Contact
The best way to get work in this field is to contact local tile contractors and ask if they're looking for apprentices. Also, International Union of Bricklayers and Allied Craftsmen, International Masonry Institute Apprenticeship and Training, 815 15th Street NW, Washington, DC 20005.

Timekeeping and Payroll Clerk

Low Down

These clerks make sure that employees' paychecks are paid on time and are accurate. The timekeeping clerk hands out and collects time cards each pay period. They review work charts, time cards and time sheets to make sure that they're accurate. Part of their job is to keep abreast of any employer payroll changes and to inform managers and other employers. Payroll clerks screen the time cards looking for errors. Most of their work is done on a computer. They also keep backup files and mail out tax withholding statements.

Scratch

Depends on the company and your experience. The pay is $9-$13 an hour.

Be
• Excellent with figures
• Comfortable in an office
• Able to do repetitive work
• Comfortable working on a computer
• Well organized and neat

Perks
• Many companies hire these clerks on a part-time basis (flexible hours)
• There is a lot of work in this field
• If you like working with figures this is a job for you

Bummers
• Work is tedious
• You're confined to an office
• Eyestrain
• Back and shoulder problems from sitting for long stretches

Horse's Mouth

Eva Bellinton, an actress: "I suppose what I like best about the work is I've always loved numbers and have been good with math. After auditions and acting classes this sort of work is like an escape for me. Is that weird? I don't know. There's something comfortable, secure, and I guess, real about numbers for me. So payroll work was always a fun job."

Contact

Most companies hire payroll and timekeeping clerks. The best place to find part-time work is at a temp agency. There is an abundance of this work so you shouldn't have any trouble finding some. You may want to go to a company directly and ask if they hire part-timers. There's a good chance that they do.

Tour Guide

Low Down

Tour guides take groups of people sightseeing either on foot or by bus. The tour can be as short as two hours or as long as eight or nine hours. The job includes greeting the sightseers, tours of specific places and buildings and relating any current events involving a specific area. You must memorize all the interesting and pertinent facts about each building and locale.

Scratch

$10-$25 an hour (can be much higher though)

Be
- A good communicator
- Well read and fluent about your tour
- Patient with people
- Friendly
- Multilingual (a plus, but not a necessity)

Perks
- If you love the city, it's a wonderful way to enjoy it.
- Occasionally you get tips
- You meet people from all over the world
- Occasionally you get dinner and/or theater invitations from the group
- Tours change and tourists change keeping interest up

Bummers
- It's seasonal work
- Tremendous amount of material to memorize
- People on the tour are often difficult
- Burnout
- Exhausting and stressful work

Horse's Moth

Joan Jaffe, an actress: "This job is like doing a long voice-over. The city is the star and you are the voice in the background. But there's no doubt you're always aware you're in front of an audience."

Contact

Circle Line Tours are very big in New York; tel. (212) 563-3204.

Toy Demonstrator

Low Down

Toy companies hire actors to demonstrate their new toy lines at trade shows. The actor is expected to be enthusiastic about the toy and should be a good salesman.

Scratch

Starts at about $7 an hour (commission basis available with some companies).

Be
• A dynamic salesman
• Friendly and outgoing
• Able to create "a carnival atmosphere"
• Funny and entertaining
• Convincing

Perks
• The work is fun
• You get to meet a lot of people
• Potential for travel
• Potential for advancement within the company
• Can be lucrative (if you're on commission)

Bummers
• Long hours
• Rough on your voice
• The toy you're demonstrating can be a real stinker (no sales)
• On your feet a lot
• Buyers can be difficult (and obnoxious)
• Trade shows are very noisy

Horse's Mouth

Sydelle Ginsberg, an actress: "I work the toy shows every year, I love it. I work for one of three companies that hire me. Part of the fun of this work is you get to play with toys. But in all fairness the work can be tiresome. It's generally a very long day. I've met some great people though."

Contact

There are many toy companies that hire actors for this work. The Actors Work Program and the SAG board list many of them. Although much of this work occurs when the toy show is in town, there are always companies looking for demonstrators. One such company is Catco, Inc., 529 West 42nd Street, New York, NY 10036; tel. (212) 563-6363.

Translator

Low Down

Many actors who are bilingual enjoy translation work. Both acting and translating are, after all, communication jobs. There are two fields to this work: translation and interpretation. Translation generally means oral skills. Chinese, Arabic and Japanese are the languages most in demand.

Scratch

Varies widely:
- Interpreters, $15-$45 an hour
- Translators, $13-$40 an hour

Be
- Able to translate quickly and efficiently
- Able to deal with people from other cultures
- Familiar and/or comfortable with scientific or technical material (translators)

Perks
- Meet all kinds of people
- If you work at the UN you may be part of history-making events
- The money can be good
- Flexible hours (work when you're available)
- Work is always available for good translators and interpreters

Bummers
- Interpreters need a great deal of training
- Some clients can be difficult to work with

Horse's Mouth

Danniel Dassin, an actor: "When I first came to this country (from Morocco) I did part-time translator work to help support myself. Since I speak several languages I always had work. It helped, believe me."

Contact

Recruitment Programmes Section, Office of Personnel Services, United Nations, New York, NY 10017.

Travel Agent

Low Down

Travel agents plan business and vacation trips for individuals, families, and groups. They schedule air transportation, hotel accommodations, car rentals and other matters fundamental to travel. They also consult and offer advice. Actors who do this job generally have outside sales rep jobs; that is, they work from home and on commission. The inside sales rep is generally a full-time position and is paid salary plus commission.

Scratch

Varies, depending on who you work for and where (outside or inside). The average outside rep receives three to five of the ten percent that the agency gets on the job.

Be
- Knowledgeable about world geography
- Willing to take a travel course
- Computer literate
- A good salesman
- Intuitive and able to anticipate your client's needs
- Pleasant and patient
- Capable of gaining a client's confidence

Perks
- Discount rates at hotels
- Free Fam Trips (familiarization trips) given by hotels and Chambers of Commerce to encourage travel
- There are plenty of openings in this field
- Work at home
- There are frequent promotional parties given by hotel chains

Bummers
- Indecisive customers
- Outside reps have no guaranteed income
- A sedentary job – not for active people
- There are slow periods

Horse's Mouth

Dick Rizzo, an actor: "I have always loved travel. I have a keen sense of geography and really enjoy planning trips for others. I feel I can use my acting skills to sell an area or destination to a client."

Contact

Dick Rizzo suggests that you go to your neighborhood travel agent and offer to work without pay until you learn the ropes. Then ask to work for them as an outside rep. To become certified as a travel agent: The Institute of Certified Travel Agents, 148 Lindon Street, PO Box 82-56, Wellesley, MA 02181; tel. (800) 542-4282.

Tutor

Low Down
Tutors work one-on-one with their students coaching everything from Scholastic Aptitude Test (SAT) preparation to any and all academic subjects.

Scratch
Starts at $25 per hour (plus travel and housing when required).

Be
- A college graduate
- Energetic and dynamic
- A great communicator
- Patient
- Professional and neat in appearance
- Proficient in academic area to be taught
- Willing to take exam (for tutoring agencies)

Perks
- Great money
- Travel possibilities (summers)
- Flexible hours
- Seeing students excel after tutoring

Bummers
- Difficult students
- Frustration of students who are slow learners
- Demanding clientele
- Sometimes unfair linkage of your work with student's progress

Horse's Mouth
Lise Jacobson, president and founder of Stanford Coaching: "Tutoring is among the most rewarding work any actor could ask for. I was formerly an actress and began tutoring to help support myself. After repeated requests by my students for tutoring in other subjects I realized that there was a great demand for this type of work and I founded my agency."

Contact
You can do this work privately or work through an agency. One of the best agencies in New York is Stanford Coaching, Inc.; tel. (212) 245-3888 (ask to speak to Lise Jacobson).

Vocational Assessment Coordinator

Low Down

The vocational assessment coordinator counsels potential employees at employment and career development agencies. He (she) administers standardized aptitude, interest and skill tests, evaluates the data and makes recommendations for vocational development.

Scratch

About $15 an hour.

Be
- Capable of evaluating a client's skills and aptitudes
- Well organized
- Comfortable working in an office
- Comfortable with all types of people

Perks
- Rewarding work (helping people find work)
- Meet all kinds of people on a daily basis

Bummers
- Difficult trying to evaluate and help place some people
- Clients can be difficult to work with

Horse's Mouth

Estelle Kornbluth, an actress: "I found this work very rewarding. Every day I'd go to work knowing that through my help someone would be able to get a job. And you meet some wonderful people. And the appreciation that they felt when they were finally placed, well, you could feel it!"

Contact

Many employment agencies hire vocational assessment coordinators. Look in the Yellow Pages. One company that hires people for this type of work is Multitasking Systems of New York. This company is a nonprofit organization that provides career planning, employment training and job placement to individuals living with HIV/AIDS. They hire actors who are HIV positive. You can reach them at 252 Seventh Avenue, 11th Floor, New York, NY 10001. Speak with Alan Huff, Employment Services Manager.

Waiter

Low Down

For as long as there's been actors there's been waiters. There's the old line, "So you're an actor, what restaurant do you work in?" Waiters work in restaurants, for caterers or in private homes. They set up for the meal, serve it and clean up afterwards.

Scratch

Working for caterers you earn $12-$20 per hour (plus tips). In restaurants you depend more on tips and receive a lower wage (runs from minimum wage to about $9 an hour).

Be
- Able to serve food
- Professional, friendly and organized
- Able to coordinate table orders
- Able to add bills up
- Physically dexterous
- Neat in appearance
- Properly dressed (tuxedo for caterers)

Perks
- In restaurants you receive your tips immediately
- Catering (especially private dinners) can pay quite well
- You meet all kinds of people
- In catering you work only when you're available
- In catering there are a lot of other actors and you can network
- Free meals (and with catering you can sometimes take food home)
- A good restaurant job can pay very well (expensive menu and/or drink charges)

Bummers
- On your feet a lot
- Balancing plates can be very difficult
- Kitchen accidents
- Irate customers
- Restaurants have slow nights
- Catered parties can run very late
- Catering work is seasonal and uneven

Horse's Mouth

Eileen Hauptman, an actress: "What can I say? I've worked both in restaurants and for caterers for years. I switch back and forth. In some ways catering is better. It's a one-night gig and then you're through. Plus some of the big catering parties at the Met or Museum of Modern Art are the social events of the year. I'd never get to be there on my own. Waitering is waitering."

Contact

There's always restaurant and catering work around if you're ambitious. Some caterers that hire actors almost exclusively are:

Great Performances; tel. (212) 727-2424

Caroline's; tel. (212) 956-0101

Movable Feast; tel. (718) 585-1748

White-Water Rafting Guide

Low Down

If you enjoy the adrenaline rush of white-water rafting and would love sharing that thrill with others, this may be the job for you. Each time you go out on the raft it's another excitement-filled adventure. Companies hire guides to assist the novice as well as the experienced white-water rafter. Just on the East Coast alone there are over 23 major and many smaller rivers that can be rafted. Guides are usually trained for this work in the early spring. The trip can be as short as a few hours or as long as a few days.

Scratch

$50-$100 per day.

Be
- Very comfortable doing this type of work
- A responsible and caring person who enjoys working with people
- Able to unpin rafts, handle launchings, throw ropes and perform the other skills necessary for rafting
- Enthusiastic

Perks
- An exciting adventure each time out
* Meet all kinds of interesting and fun people
- A great job for people who love the outdoors

Bummers
- Can be dangerous!
- Difficult passengers
- Seasonal work
- Even if you take the course, which costs several hundred dollars, there's no guarantee you'll get work

Horse's Mouth

Leonard Remington, an actor: "I've been a white-water rafter since I was a kid. My family used to go on outings all the time. I work (freelance) for several companies. When I need to get away, usually in August when things are slow, I just take off for a few weeks. Aside from just being in the great outdoors, it's a great way to make some money. You have to see the looks on people's faces their first time out to understand why it's such a fun job."

Contact

American Whitewater Affiliation, 146 North Brockway, Palatine, IL 60067. They put out a magazine called *American Whitewater* which lists the information you'll need.

Wine Steward (Sommelier)

Low Down

If you are a connoisseur of fine wines and are comfortable working in distinguished restaurants this may be the job for you. Actors often enjoy working as a sommelier because of the role they get to play. Attending wine tastings and continuously reading books and magazines about wine tasting are essential.

Scratch

Varies widely depending on the restaurant, the city and the location. Full-time wine stewards earn up to $60,000 a year (includes tips and salary).

Be
- Extremely knowledgeable about wine
- A real showman (without being stuffy)
- A pleasant, easygoing person, able to get along with all types of customers and restaurant clientele
- Able to serve wine properly, open a bottle correctly and take an order elegantly

Perks
- Even on a part-time basis the money can be very good
- Can lead to teaching courses in the subject
- There is a lot of "theater" to the job; you are playing a specific role
- Get to meet some very fine and interesting people

Bummers
- The training for this type of work is extensive
- Customers can be competitive, challenging your taste and knowledge
- Managements at exclusive restaurants and hotels are demanding
- Conforming to an actor's schedule can be difficult

Horse's Mouth

Jean Moniel, an actor: "I found that the best way for me to do this work in restaurants or hotels was to give up acting for that period of time. You generally have to be in early to do pre-set and special order. Some of the better caterers now hire wine stewards on a freelance basis for their better affairs."

Contact

Sommelier Society of America, 201 East 25th Street, New York, NY 10010; tel. (212) 679-4190.

Wire Transfer Worker

Low Down

When people or corporations want to transfer money they use the services of a company that offers wire transfers. The wire transfer worker interviews the client and completes the transaction by sending the funds to the receiver. Wire transfers can be made anywhere in the world.

Scratch

From $7 to $12 an hour. Some companies offer health benefits.

Be
- Possessed of good phone skills
- Able to use a calculator
- Equipped with good handwriting
- Able to take information on the phone efficiently
- Knowledgeable about money conversion

Perks
- You may have pleasant ongoing phone relationships with different people
- Many companies offer benefits (even part-time)
- Hours are flexible

Bummers
- Mistakes occur and create problems
- Stuck in an office
- Pressure at times
- Some customers may be difficult

Horse's Mouth

John Fixler, an actor: "I enjoy this type of work. It really can be fun. You get to know some of the people at some of the companies very well. Yeah, there's sometimes pressure, but generally it's a pleasant way to make some extra money; plus the health benefits are worth a lot these days."

Contact

Call any of the wire transfer services listed in the Yellow Pages. Federal credit unions also hire wire transfer workers. Western Union; tel. (800) 325-6000.

Yoga Instructor (Private and Group)

Low Down

If you're adept at yoga and feel confident that you can teach the asanas (exercises) this may be something to look into. You can teach either privately, in people's homes, or in groups, at companies, or organizations. Yoga helps people to relax, concentrate better, and connect with their spiritual center.

Scratch

Private, about $45 per session; Group, about $100 to $150 per session.

Be
- An expert at Yoga (being certified is a real plus)
- Sensitive to your client's medical profile
- Sensitive to your client's emotional needs
- Patient and gentle
- Observant
- A positive reinforcer and motivator

Perks
- Very rewarding spiritually
- Hours are flexible
- Meet all kinds of people
- Change lives for the better

Bummers
- Some people are difficult to motivate
- Client's are sometimes late for their sessions (throws your schedule off)
- Difficult clients

Horse's Mouth

Lynn Rabinowitz, actress and certified yoga instructor: "This work is tremendously rewarding. Seeing people learn to relax, get comfortable with their bodies and themselves, it doesn't get much better than that. I've been teaching for about 11 years and everyday I still learn new things from my clients about spiritual growth. I heartily recommend that you look into this work."

Contact

This is self-starter kind of work. You must place ads on bulletin boards and let people know that you're in business. Contact different companies and offer your services to their employees.